TODD VICKERS

THE PARADOX OF SELF-REALIZATION

The Paradox of Self-Realization
2nd Edition
By Todd Vickers

Copyright Page

Content Copyright 2019 © Vickers Publications. All Rights Reserved.

I am revising this book for several reasons. First, while I love and stand behind the content of the book, it deserves more justice than my skill allowed for 20 years ago. The point I wanted to make then is the same as today: to share the knowledge and experiences that have benefited me greatly. I also want to encourage scrutiny of unnecessary and oft ignored wishful thinking and superstition that tends to adhere to methods, such as meditation. When we endow any practice with qualities it does not possess, we create a problem that might obscure the real benefit of the practice.

I often focus on sexual topics within which we need to be extremely honest. We would be hard pressed to find a topic better than sex to expose the habits of the mind. For example, when a man falls in love and begins to imagine a future with the other person, in the imagined story stands a mental sense of self. If marriage is imagined, then he may see himself at the altar in a tuxedo with his beloved. That sense of self never existed outside the mind, yet it induces strong emotions and we unconsciously (habitually) treat our mental sense of self as if it is real. This concept of self is a problem when we take it to be real. We might ignore and distort the facts around us for the sake of trying to secure the comfort of that mental self. I suggest that, as long as we, individually or as a society, remain willfully ignorant about something as important as sexuality, then our motives for doing are bound up in this imaginary self. From this mistake, we undoubtedly gain insight into why we turn away from and distort other important and difficult facts, both personal and social. We should not be wasting precious time and energy trying to defend an imagined self. Nor should we sacrifice our choices and ability to adapt in exchange for the temporary and self-satisfying comfort induced while treating a fictional self as real.

This book was my first attempt at writing for the public. I made a mistake in rushing it to print before it was ready. In this second edition, I've reduced the redundancies, emotional arguments, and vague spiritual language within it and added more concrete examples that serve the points better. Vagueness invites readers to see what they want to see within statements. Such language drives skeptics crazy. I am not being derisive with the word 'skeptic.' The skeptic has a special place of honor in subjective matters because skeptics reveal value by showing where room for doubt exists. Confidence won't make a house of cards stable. Emphasis is not evidence. One who upsets the cards is not dangerous, but trusting a house of cards sure is! The faults (esoteric language, grammatical indulgence, and redundancy) in the original book took the reader for granted. I have applied the pruning shears and reorganized the book. These changes, coupled with luck and whatever skills I've gathered along the way, I hope, will make the content more accessible to you, dear readers.

INTRODUCTION TO THE FIRST EDITION

I have written this book because I have found the desire to share what is beautiful and helpful to be compelling. Endless opportunities exist by which to discover and unfold our understanding of ourselves and the world. New understanding embraces what we did not previously know. After all, the world continues to change, that is, recreate itself moment to moment. The subject matter of this book involves risk. Early on, I received criticism from an editor. She reviewed the work for about 10 minutes and said she wouldn't work with it. She explained that her path was about reclaiming innocence (whatever that means) and that this book contained so much about the human shadow that she wouldn't have anything to do with it. She then asked my birthday and pigeonholed me using Chinese astrology.

I considered trying to say things differently, but that seemed pretentious. Sometimes, I use strong language, but this type of talk has benefited me throughout my life. Plenty of smarmy and patronizing spiritual communications exist and I have chosen to write in a different way. Don't get me wrong, I like light-hearted and joyful communications as much as the next person, but that is not all there is to say. Some of us feel hurt, disappointed, and, even, betrayed by the spiritual teachings that emphasize love and joy, but do not help us when we run face first into unfortunate circumstances or must face our own destructive beliefs or habits. Any tendency to create useless suffering for ourselves and others, I call the human shadow. The selfishness that is so often found in relationships is a good example, people are often valued only as means to another end, rather than ends unto themselves. The darkness of selfishness, fear, ambition, competition, vanity, and desire for power all hides easily behind a beautiful, idealistic, and flower decorated exterior. I do not claim that the shadow is wrong; it is a part of life and the desire for a truthful life is what I mean when I use the word 'sacred.' However, if we pretend that we don't have this destructive shadow, then we won't account for what that shadow is doing. When we look at subjective methods, be they spiritual paths or therapy, we see this shadow and, ironically, much of the work that people do is to try to run away from or explain away this shadow. However, this shadow isn't nearly as scary as what people do when they try to conceal it.

Nothing can be said that is as profane as what is hidden inside and won't be said. For me, it is not enough just to pay lip service to the love of truth. I live it and hope that this book reaches out to others who have the same passion. Perhaps, we'll meet beyond these pages, but, regardless, be warned, such communications involve risk and, speaking for myself, I won't always come out smelling like a rose. For example, I spoke to a woman who never felt sexually met by her lover; she spent years hoping that it would get better. It was obvious to me that she continually felt pain over this issue. Shortly after this conversation, I heard that she planned to marry this man. I felt compelled to ask her what the hell she was doing. After all, this was her life! I said some things that hurt her fiancée's feelings. This type of thing happens because withholding something that might spare a friend misery seems to me like hanging a friend out to dry. It's worth the risk.

Under the guise of 'sharing,' people often say many things without accounting for the moral and emotional impact of that sharing on other human beings. The assumption that a friend will agree is often wrong. I criticize the judgment of friends if I see a good reason to do so, especially if it involves doubtful beliefs and useless suffering. Some friends hardly speak to me anymore due to such conversations. Many social prohibitions suggest that we're not supposed to confront someone in pain, particularly if that pain involves beliefs, sex, or both.

To me, the sharing of any pain is literally a sharing of pain and all sensitive people, especially when they feel love for the person sharing the pain, feel the pain in some way. Typically, the person talking does not account for what his or her pain is doing to others. He or she might abuse another person's empathy, especially if the emotion being conveyed intimidates the other into not speaking for fear of a consequence. Such communication implicitly suggests that the listener 'walk on eggshells' rather than question what is being shared or scrutinize the beliefs of the sharing person. In order to illustrate this point, consider that a person you love holds his or her hand over a hot stove, while whimpering in pain. Anyone near this person would probably feel horror observing the burning flesh of another human being. Now, let us assume that, in this situation, social manners won't allow you to speak directly about what is happening because your loved one may feel hurt or belittled. Obeying this strange sentimentality, everyone present must talk around the problem and the pain, possibly stating how great the situation would be if it were different, perhaps in a better world. In this extreme example, we can see that any sane person would demand that the sufferer take his or her hand away from the damn stove! To be unable to make this demand would be maddening, especially if you feel great love for the person who is suffering. Most people would agree that it would be ok to try to stop the suffering in the situation with the hot stove, but might abandon such a standard when the pain is emotional, spiritual, sexual, or financial or when it involves threats to their own interests.

There are things that we aren't supposed to say (at least not to someone's face) because it is none of our business or seems presumptuous. Returning to the woman above who married at the expense of her sexual joy, she knows, as all of my friends do, that, among other things, I view sex, wild or mild, as important and worthy of great kindness and respect. Moreover, benign sexual choices deserve a strong defense, particularly in a society that often ignores or rejects many benign forms of sexuality. That same society has produced many educated people who not only lie about their sexuality, but also ignore facts like STDs. When this woman came to me professing a desire for relief, expressing great pain because of her unfulfilled sexuality, my compassion made me become a kindred ally. After all, I have known similar pain and made changes for the better. I hope to encourage others who are willing to live our sexual imperatives with great integrity; learn, admit, and correct mistakes; and consciously invite more freedom for others and themselves. I feel saddened when the prospect of living in such a way is devalued out of prejudice. Never tell a man who is doing something that it cannot be done. This peeve of mine doesn't armor me against feeling another's pain and I feel no consolation in being smug when the obvious consequences of such pretentiousness come to pass. I am not saying that there is anything wrong with people sharing their pain if that pain is shared in a circumstance that welcomes and receives what others might speak in return. I'm not saying someone cannot criticize a response of mine if he or she sees a fault. I'm saying that it is both ignorant and arrogant to simply dismiss help. If someone is not willing to listen to a response to his or her pain, then that person's choice to share is more like dumping garbage. Such conversations are intense and intimate. If people later act as if the conversation never took place, then it is both astonishing and painfully tragic. My responsibility in such conversations is that I won't reject such risk because it is part of affection and part of a life well-lived, but, like any effort, it disappoints when the time spent trying to communicate seems wasted for nothing.

Sex and sexuality are topics that reveal unfounded beliefs and are touchy subjects. Being both fact-based and intense, sexuality itself often shatters the delusions that we have about it. Again, I suggest that moving closer to the truth is the only thing worthy of the name 'sacred' and that makes the shattering of delusions sacred. Anything that prevents the reality loss we call delusion also deserves the name 'sacred.' Sex is one of the three big illusion killers. The others being death and money. Other minor disappointments, like losing a competition or the destruction of some valued object, also pose challenges to our beliefs. We can consciously choose to welcome the truth instead of being blindsided by brutal facts contrary to our beliefs when life forces those facts upon us. Many people talk about sexual anxiety, pain, and disappointment. Often, this pain rests on real or imagined deprivation. Sexuality is not wrong. I don't believe sexuality is responsible for any mistakes of judgment and it's unfair to fault sex for our dubious beliefs. However, it's important to criticize beliefs about sexuality and any irresponsible behavior that involves violence, coercion, recklessness, or deceit.

Moving from sex to life in general, I find it repugnant to condone bullshit with silence. A person in pain as a result of some unquestioned belief may feel that he or she is doing something to resolve the pain when he or she shares it. A discussion of pain is supposed to be significant or, at least, intimate. Yet, the pain can continue for years, maybe even a lifetime, because the belief still stands. Through repetition, beliefs become unconscious habits. Like tying our shoes or chewing gum, we need not think about an unconscious belief to enable it to automatically guide our conduct. A person in the grips of such a habit may talk critically about the habit when he or she is feeding the inertia of habits, talking about a habit is not the same as breaking the habit. If he or she won't go beyond talking in order to consciously alter his or her thinking and conduct, then his or her sharing about the habit may work against him or her because it pretends to be problem-solving. Like an alcoholic or smoker talks about stopping the habit, but never quits. The words may be spoken with great feeling, but they can actually mean little or nothing and, in this way, such a conversation becomes self-deceptive and misleads others as well.

Beliefs, habits, expectations, prejudices, and routines overlap in that they involve predictions and would have no value if they did not. We decide the courses of our lives and also impact the lives of others based on such predictions. Seeking out falsehoods and mistakes in beliefs, habits, or anything our predictions are built upon is a responsibility needed for a conscious life. If we squander years in our own unnecessary suffering because we neglect this responsibility, then we undoubtedly become a cause of pain for others. We won't get those years back or be able to undo the consequences of that futile misery. Those years are the price paid for living in the inertia of mental habits. When a person finally sees these beliefs, when he or she wakes up to the bonds of such habits, then he or she might feel how much he or she has lost by living on autopilot and half dead. One of the habits of mind is the way that we conceive of ourselves and I repeatedly reference this identity throughout this book as a source of many mistakes. Awakening doesn't free us from responsibility, it frees us into responsibility.

I am looking for and hoping to find others who wish to wake up from sleepy, life-consuming habits. I am interested in making a space where many different types of trial, error, and discovery are welcome, for those who choose to live their own lives and not just obey and rebel in a mechanical fashion to the popular beliefs of their cultures. Waking up, as I define it, is the summit of human adaptation. It is not knowing all the right answers, that would be being an automaton. Waking up includes conscious trial and error in thought and practice in recognition of what we don't know. It includes people with all kinds of different ways of being, different kinds of work, and different ways of thinking. Waking up includes people who are sexual and those who are not, people who are into monogamy and those individuals who go far beyond those limits. Anyone can wake up.

The subjective inquiry, including meditation, that helps us in our learning and discovery, is not simply a quest for an altered state, pomp, ritual, pursuit of pleasure, or a concept of enlightenment. Self-inquiry often arises as a response to discontent, which is the engine of human adaptation or maladaptation. Consciousness is the essence of successful adaptation because we cease to identify ourselves with the products of our minds and realize that no threat exists to us to see the flaws in any product of thought, including our identities. We begin by simply meeting reality with new access to our bodies and minds. Think of our capacities as a box of one hundred color crayons. If we habitually confine ourselves to just thirty colors, the fact that we have several choices does not liberate us from the oppression of our habits. Such liberation helps us in any effort to find better ways to live and help others do the same. Self-inquiry may (and hopefully does) include other people interested in living as close to the truth as they can get. Such people not only share mutual joys and support, but can also see into our blind spots and help us avoid useless suffering. Such discovery cannot be lived inside some routine, spiritual or otherwise. Life is not a place where we can control experiments. I'm critical of those individuals who trash trial and error attempts at life. After all, many of the benefits of modern life that we take for granted became preferred alternatives to backward methods and beliefs that existed in the past. Someone somewhere thought it would be worthwhile to treat women and children like human beings instead of cattle. That was a radical idea that remains radical today in more backward countries. We owe such trial and error respect for what it has accomplished. Not everyone wants to pursue something better or take the risk. That is their choice, but that does not make the willingness to try something new a bad thing, even when it fails. Life can be a discovery beyond how we habitually know ourselves and the world.

In this book, I also challenge established ideas about spirituality, which tends to bring about various temperatures of indignation in those individuals who have adopted the spiritual beliefs in question. If someone sees a flaw in what I say, then he or she should try to expose it. I would do the same in his or her place (e.g., I make statements about spiritual awakening). People have many ideas about awakening, enlightenment, and wisdom. Clearly, some of these ideas are absurd. For example, a person who is wise is supposed to have gray hair and a beard. As Erasmus pointed out in the 15th century, these qualities are common among both men and goats. Enlightened people are supposed to behave like...well...an awakened person and the ideas about what that is range from close to the truth to fantastically wrong. We bring our preconceived ideas with us when we become seekers. If a person comes from a Buddhist background, then he or she has a Buddhist standard and will look for a Buddhist explanation. People invest years and lives into these beliefs and, when some guy like me comes along and says "Hey, I'm awake, and here is what I have to say," that guy is going to meet resistance.

I know what self-realization is: it is the disillusion of identity itself and the recognition that thought gets mistaken for more than thought, be it concerning the world or ourselves. Many thinkers understand the limits of thought about the world, but they are in the dark about the same conceptual nature of the self. It is good that people are skeptical, especially about subjective matters; that will help them from being led into a spiritual rut that they can't get out of. There are lots of teachers out there and one must be able to separate those teachers who help from those teachers who don't. What surprises me is how it often seems impressive to be a great seeker of truth and spend one's life in all types of spiritual gymnastics while trying to awaken. That situation is considered respectable. However, to realize anything true and then say it without reference to some acknowledged higher authority, perhaps scripture, someone dead, or a famous teacher, that situation is considered arrogant and ostentatious. Apparently, the way to keep everyone calm is to not awaken or share if it is contrary to popular belief. If I say something flawed or extravagant, then the strength or weakness of the statement should be based on the content, the known facts, and reasoning. Those standards have nothing to do with credentials, age, race, or any pigeonhole, including upstart, charlatan, and sex addict, that someone may choose to assign to me. Awakening is acceptable, whether it is accepted or not.

Let's make a distinction between seeking and discovering. A seeker is seeking something. Often that something is experiential and, like it or not, every experience is fleeting. Moreover, any sincere seeker may not be making a distinction between fictional mind stuff inducing experiences within them and the facts around them that may be entirely different. This includes any meaning we add to the concept of awakening. That is a huge discovery. Awakening is not a composite of all the spiritual ideas that appeal to or induce our sentiments. When we wake up, we cease to treat the meaning we add to events as if that meaning is true and, instead, treat meaning as what it is: passing thought that could more or less represent the facts. Life continually reveals itself to us without being bound to any particular meaning we add. We begin to adapt our thinking to life, instead of struggling to get life to fit into our thinking. We see the people and events around us, including those experiences labeled spiritual, with a new clarity that's not bound to salvaging our identity at any cost. All of life is being in the presence of truth; it is our thinking that so often causes problems, not because thought is bad, but because we treat our thinking as if it were fact when we are so often wrong.

I criticize a lot of ideologies without replacing them with a new ideology other than a general openness. This action leaves people with a sense of free fall that can be uncomfortable at first. I want to leave the reader with himself or herself when he or she is done reading, literally. This message suggests removing arbitrary limits imposed by a mere concept of our own identities. What someone does afterward is his or her own discovery and should not be an imitation of my life or discovery. This book is for people whose spiritual needs are unmet by beliefs or practices of rituals and techniques, or, perhaps, for those individuals who haven't had the opportunity to even inquire into themselves or their beliefs.

I can't count how many hours I've spent in meditation or being fascinated by altered states, what people call spiritual experiences. I've met people considered spiritual masters, more than I will name in this book. I spent 10 years in many kinds of therapy, both traditional and non-traditional, exploring family issues and the emotional shocks that I experienced growing up. Digressing, I have reconciled with my parents in love. I have their respect and admiration, not because they agree with my lifestyle (they don't), but because I am no longer a drugged out, thieving, angry, miserable, arrogant, pain in the ass. My father told me once that he wouldn't have been surprised to find me with my brains blown out, prior to this change. I became a seeker because I became aware of useless pain I created for others and myself. My parents are happy with the changes that I've made and, for that reason, they don't disrespect my life choices. In fact, my father occasionally asks me some profound questions. I don't think my father understands much of what I say to him about such matters; however, he listens closely and considers my answer until he is satisfied that the conversation can go no further. I stand on the shoulders of my parents and the generations that came before them. I have learned from their mistakes and destructive habits of mind. They are a big reason why I began seeking the truth. They are as much responsible for my awakening as any help I've received. My father repeats, on occasion, a remark that he made in my infancy, "That kid will do anything and God help us if he goes in the wrong direction."

I came into this world being intense and you may notice this intensity in my writing. I'm sharing what benefited me. If a person needs something else, then I support wholeheartedly his or her need. I personally have followed the impulse to something truer, both before and after my awakening. It was this impulse that led and opened me to many previously hidden good fortunes. I don't have a monopoly on good fortune and anyone who says he or she does is a liar. Fortune is circumstantial and many circumstances are beyond the control of those individuals affected. A tsunami washes away the rich, poor, crass, artisans, the innocent and the guilty. When it comes to good circumstances, it may be that we don't create opportunities, but, instead, we simply stop habitually destroying them. Destructive habits of the mind, like a bondage to an identity or prejudice, impose limits upon us and simply ignore many of our capacities, both good and bad. If someone's impulse leads him or her in a direction that seems to be contradictory to what I am saying, then I say good luck. I know that you must follow the truth where it leads you (that is what I would do) and you will do it in circumstances that I may never know anything about. I wish for you both good fortune and the sense to recognize the good things actually available to you.

It may seem crass to say, but I also hope that I sell books to support this work and myself. I say that so that you know I am for real. I need to survive in this world in order to articulate the vision that I offer and it would be nice if that effort would support itself. I have been working since I got my first job delivering newspapers at the age of 10 and I will continue to work for as long as I need. However, some work is worth more than others.

BEING WITH LIFE

(Life is not obligated to our beliefs about it)

The ability to adapt to changing events is present in, but willfully ignored by most people, especially when one is not presented with an immediate consequence that would punish our infidelity to the truth. This is often called wishful thinking or, more pointedly, delusion. Our ability to adapt to facts is not nurtured as it might be in a better world because this ability has the tendency to reveal unsettling truths about ourselves, others including those in power. When we refuse to be with life as it is, for whatever reason, we suffer because bullshitting ourselves is painful. Facts will punish us sooner or later and later is, often, much worse. If we grasp a hot kettle, then the sooner we realize the mistake, the better. There is harshness that arises from facing facts, but the reward of more choices is, by far, superior to denying or changing facts. If we refuse to see or distort facts habitually to spare our beliefs, then we enter a trap and the misery we hoped to avoid becomes amplified. Willful ignorance robs us of many choices.

The facts most difficult to face are the aspects of ourselves contrary to our habituated identity. In therapeutic groups, I've witnessed a tendency to sugarcoat what is considered objectionable aspects of ourselves, such as anger, lust, selfishness, and dishonesty. These aspects are sometimes explained as reactions or defense mechanisms developed in childhood to survive the environment. Now, granted, this type of explanation has a certain plausibility. It is also comforting to blame selfishness, dishonesty, and hurtful behaviors on painful childhood events and deprivation. Indeed, that is where many troubling habits of the mind begin. However, this type of explanation creates an excuse for the suffering that these uglier aspects cause ourselves and others.

A woman who experienced pain and deprivation in her past sought my advice on how to deal with her difficult financial situation. She had years of experience with therapy and motivational groups, seminars and workshops, life coaching, and spiritual retreats and journeys to the feet of gurus. She accrued an incredible amount of debt and, ironically, continually borrowed money to continue to 'work on herself.' Now, when she asked me for help, I warned her that I felt bound to speak frankly. She approved and agreed to do as I instructed as an experiment to see if it would help. I told her that she was lazy, but that there was no problem with that. If she could just be with that and accept responsibility for the kind of life that laziness creates, then she might be able to relax into herself and enjoy it. If she could not do that, then she needed a job. She was offended that I would say such a thing, but I felt that I couldn't truthfully say anything else. She then told me of her idea to borrow several thousand dollars from a man who was interested in her romantically for the purpose of advertising her real estate business. I asked her how many hours she was willing to work and she said no more than four hours per day. I told her that it was dishonest of her to manipulate and borrow from a man to advertise a business that she wasn't willing to make time for, even if she attracted more business. I knew of her heavy debt and her willingness to borrow from other lovers and would-be lovers that she never paid back. If she wasn't willing to work, then she probably wouldn't be able to pay back this new 'patsy' or be able to thrive, let alone pay off her debts. She immediately stopped talking to me and went back to therapy. There has been no change in her situation in the years that have since passed except that she started drinking after a long period of abstinence.

I can't say what would have happened to the woman referenced above if she had listened to me, but I can say that I responded to the simple facts of her life without deference to sentiment. She refused to live with her reality and opted for a more complex solution, which hadn't yielded results in the past. She found consolation in the identity of being a spiritual seeker who 'worked on herself' to be a better person. She saw herself according to her intentions and life imposed upon her the factual consequences of her actions. In her case, the seeking became avoidance and formed the chains of her self-made prison. The facts of her life exposed her, but she could have been just as trapped if she were an heiress with more money than she could spend. The issue here is living in life as it is. If our spirituality or self-exploration can't help us adapt to life as it is, then I doubt the benefits of such self-improvement.

Again, we can't take responsibility for any aspect of our multidimensional life that we refuse to acknowledge. We end up pretentiously disowning objectionable aspects of ourselves, as if that were really possible. This disowning is often called denial. I don't like the word 'denial' because it suggests that people do not know that they are turning away from facts. The woman above knew enough about a comfortable delusion to avoid my suggestions. I prefer the word 'pretense' over denial in this case because pretense not only requires effort, but also suggests that we know we are doing it.

Bad habits related to thoughts and beliefs affect our lives from behind the scenes, like computer viruses running in the background. It's like we're engaging in a covert war against ourselves and our life energy and attention are devoted to maintaining the struggle. We remain in our more or less familiar, conditional, fragmented, and limited identities because we defend them with emotional insistence that we are who we think we are. The woman mentioned above wasn't clear about the problem of identity, but she was confident that she was not lazy or manipulative. Her situation grew worse by investing her money and time into spiritual theories and therapy that did nothing more than pretend to explain or rationalize her self-deluding beliefs. Those authorities profited off of her ongoing self-deception and her two children suffered in poverty.

We have vague ideas about what a healthy or normal person is as well as what enlightenment is. These ideals are suggested each time the words unhealthy, abnormal i.e., chemically imbalanced and delusional are brought up. These words suggest an opposite of healthy, normal, or balanced. This language can be exploited to be dangled as bait toward an unrealistic goal in front of suggestible people. A vague ideal self in a vague ideal circumstance has nothing to do with the awakening I'm discussing. An ideal always remains conceptual; however, one might ask whether spiritual liberation is supposed to free us from the objectionable and neurotic. Liberation is not freedom from the problems of life, but freedom in the midst of anything life throws our way. The truth is that realizing that identity is nothing more than a useful fiction frees us from the delusional bondage of that fiction. There are aspects of life that are not pretty, but we need not make it worse by believing falsehoods to protect a fictional identity. When we recognize this fact, it is much easier to adapt to the world around us because any idea of self is seen to be just an abstraction and not who we actually are.

THE DISILLUSIONED

My first real disillusionment came with the death of my sister. At the age of 19, she wrecked her car. I was nine-years-old and my last words to her were in the anger of a petulant little brother. She was my favorite person in the world. I wanted to believe that she could hear me in another life and I wanted the ministers who consoled my family to be right that there was a future life. Regardless, I saw that they didn't really know and that shocked me. Not that they admitted that they didn't know, they didn't. I saw that there was no way that they could know what happened after death and that all of their consolations about a future life rested on hot air. This disillusionment made me angry.

I turned 30 in 1998, so my youth was firmly entrenched in the 1980s. My generation listened to punk rock, heavy metal, and techno music. We were the first to learn about AIDS and we had no idea how that disease would affect all of us. Generation X was probably exposed, via the media, to more double-talk, hypocrisy, and plain old stupidity than any other generation before it. In the past, it might have taken 30 or 40 years to find out that some public figure lied to us, but the media continuously exposed more corruption faster to us. Our institutions of law and government often appeared to be nothing more than a circus of profanity. Sexual hypocrisy was (and still is) so prominent that, to not see it, one must have on a blindfold. The Catholic Church continues to settle cases of rape by their priests. Politicians and evangelists caught with prostitutes bow their heads in shame. Today, on the Internet, you can view everything sexual from erotica to the most shocking things you can imagine, all from the privacy of your own living room. What about New Age Spirituality? Wasn't that going to be the answer? I knew a young woman who quite sincerely went to a channeler to seek answers to her questions. This "channeler of the higher self" told her that the reason she was unfulfilled was that her father sexually assaulted her as a child. She had no memories whatever of such an event and felt quite surprised. She nonetheless assumed that this statement was the truth, after all, it was being channeled from her 'higher self'. This young woman, then about 22-years-old, went and confronted her father with this revelation. He felt crushed. She explained to him how she came about this information and suggested that they both go and see the channeler together.

Her father felt eager to meet the person who made the accusation. (That must have been one shaky channeler that day!) This channeler revealed that the higher self knew that there needed to be a meeting on a deep level between this young woman and her father, so the higher self 'created' the story to open an opportunity. The question as to whether the incest actually happened in a past life remained open. The father felt satisfied because it seemed to resolve the issue with his daughter and didn't seek revenge on the channeler for that reason. If you ask me, the whole thing stinks. I must give the channeler credit for some fancy footwork, but I don't think this type of help is truly helpful. People trust such authority and it's often a rude awakening when the authority is wrong or, worse, deceitful.

At any time, life itself might disillusion us. One evening in 1991, I slept in the passenger seat of my brother's car while we approached a patch of black ice. We entered a canyon around dusk. As the temperature lowered, ice began to form on water that had melted during the day. My brother obliviously drove with the cruise control on. We were doing about 65 mph. I woke up just as the car lost control and said "here we go!" I knew that I couldn't do anything. We skidded sideways and my brother over-corrected, so we crossed the center line. I saw a big Ford heading right for my door. We struck hard and it hit us just behind my door between the rear seat and the trunk. The shock sent the car careening out of control toward a cliff that dropped into a river. My brother had his eyes closed and the brakes floored at this point. We stopped with our front tires teetering over the cliff and the car high-centered. Thankfully, everyone walked away. The car was totaled, the rear end was ripped apart, and all four tires were flat. It doesn't matter how much money we have in the bank, how much insurance we have, or how many mantras we have chanted. We exist in a physically changing, real world and we don't know how the day's events will turn out. If the Ford had hit just a few inches closer to me, I would have been injured terribly or killed. Death can catch us at any time; the rich can become poor, the healthy can and do become sick, commitments are broken, and, sometimes, we can't even imagine the reason why things are the way they are. Reality isn't ever bound to our capacity to understand it. Spend a night watching the news and you will see what I am talking about. When I say capacity, I mean what we can do as we are in this moment limited only by the mechanical bounds of our bodies and minds. I do not mean potential which is future oriented.

There is nothing wrong with trying to avoid unnecessary pain, saving money, or having insurance. The idea that we can manage events is naive in many ways as we don't even manage the symbiotic organisms in our bodies that we need to live in a healthy manner. Bad things even happen to people with the most enviable of circumstances. We do the best that we can, with the knowledge we possess, and, still, it's a crapshoot. If we are lucky, we experience some good fortune that will lead us along a truer path. Not just to avoid the useless misery that we create when we believe things that are untrue, but also so that we don't miss the good things our own life is offering us. It is wiser to bet on our own awareness than on some idea of the way life should be. If you are curious about this type of recognition, meet with a person like me, who knows that one's identity is fiction. I meet people for this reason, but I am not everyone's cup of tea. I don't believe self-realization (the recognition that identity is a fiction that comes and goes in our awareness) is anything beyond the scope of mortals, it's not special, though it seems quite rare.

When I was a spiritual seeker, I guarded myself against people who pretended to be spiritual. The truth is that after I realized the awareness that I'm talking about here, I can now see that people are pretending to be unenlightened and they are denying much of what life offers. I'm not saying that life offers anyone more choices when identity is realized to be fiction. I'm saying that, once we realize any identity is fiction, our vision is not arbitrarily tunneled in an attempt to sustain ideas of the self. The disillusioned are people who have had their beliefs destroyed by something true. They cannot pretend that they don't see and feel the shadows that we hide. They know that people masturbate. They know that people cheat on their spouses. They know that people say one thing and do another. Things have always been like this. Hypocrisy is nothing new. Just ask a Native American about all of the treaties that America has broken.

One might wonder if apathy is born of betrayal. If that is so, then why does apathy affect so many people and their kids, including those individuals who have all of the privileges? Perhaps because they can't live the lies that the previous generations have perpetuated. Maybe we know too much to be happy with the lies that we have inherited from the past. When a person has done what he or she was "supposed" to do, materially or spiritually, to be happy and then realizes that he or she isn't happy and may be miserable, he faces disillusionment. There is a particular type of pain that comes from trying to make an idea that can't fulfill us fulfilling. The phrase 'vicious circle' comes to mind.

I am not saying that what these disillusioned people are seeing is all of the truth. However, they do see the rationalization and minimizing of consequences used to excuse the typical beliefs about life that are peddled to consumers. Religion is just one of those ideas. The bullshit is going on all around and they see it. They may not know what the truth is, but they know much of what they see and hear isn't it or, at least, isn't all of it. How do you explain to a young girl that many of the supermodels on the covers of the magazines that she reads can't menstruate because their bodies are so malnourished? The models starve themselves to look sexy and, as a result of this self-mortification, they can't function in a healthy, sexual way. Such ideas about what is sexy show an insane double message. Facts like these bring disillusionment. It is no wonder that so much apathy exists in the lives of younger people. It is stark raving crazy out in the world and the suffering is immeasurable. Yes, we live longer. Yes, technology progresses and there are some social changes for the better, but those facts do not reconcile the twisted beliefs spoon-fed to most people through their families and cultures.

What do I have to say to the younger generations? If you are blessed/cursed with a thirst for the truth, then that is what I call a divine discontent because anything less is unsatisfactory. Desire for truth, to be as close to truth as our senses and understanding can possibly allow, is not a desire to meet some imagined god or for a life after the body rots, but an openness and invitation to the truth, whatever it may be, even if that truth shatters our most treasured beliefs.

If we are sensitive enough, then we notice that something painful and unnecessary abides in the circus that is going on around us under the guise of normal. We, on the whole, blithely pollute the air we breathe and the water we drink. We overpopulate the planet and, thereby, foster poverty, starvation, war, and disease. It is not a large stretch to suspect that we, as a species, are capable of doing better, but progress always begins with a minority and often faces opposition and even oppression.

If you choose a more conscious life, meaning living less automatically, habitually, routinely, and with less imitation of others, then you will have to shoulder the responsibilities that previous generations haven't had to shoulder. I'm not saying that you will have to reinvent the wheel, but consider if all of our ancestors simply followed the dots, then we would not have progressed as a species. Adaptation means reckoning with the real world, not the virtual representation of it in our minds, though those minds may be largely helpful. Pretending that we aren't polluting our own water, when we are, is unacceptable and ill-adapted to our needs as living beings. Personally, if we can't be honest about things like our own sexuality, how will we, as a species, even hope to deal with an issue like climate change? To get conscious, we must stop blindly following the dots laid out for us by others, stop living in the habits of our minds, and begin to adapt to the people and world around us.

The same is true of spirituality. Many beliefs sold as spiritual are doubtful and misleading, regardless of the intention of the people who advocate such beliefs. There is no belief that can't go into the crucible of scrutiny. This risking of our beliefs, including beliefs about ourselves, is a responsibility many wish to avoid. Instead of explaining away why a marriage failed, why not ask if marriage itself is necessary?

The responsibility is on the individual to weigh the differences between reality and fiction and our leaders may harm or help. No matter how good an idea seems, particularly if it won't perform as promised, let's not be bound to it. Sometimes, a disillusionment can be so great that it leaves us with absolutely no place to stand because what we believed and tried failed and we don't know what to do next. I know how hard this situation can be. In that painful state, we can become conscious of something in us untouched by the pain of disillusionment. This aspect (for a lack of a better word) is untouched by any feeling, thought, or experience. It is the source from which all thoughts, feelings, and perceptions spring forth. It is our awareness itself. While we are in bliss or agony, we are, at the same time, utterly free. The feelings or experiences we have don't change the awareness that feelings come and go within, even when our lives may be utterly transformed in dramatic ways. I am not asking you to simply adopt this statement about awareness as a belief; the abandonment of responsibility and acceptance of beliefs on the word of another plagues the world. If we don't have reason to think something true, then we should keep hold of our doubts. We know feelings, thoughts, and, even, perceptions mislead us at times, so how can we prove anything about the awareness discussed above? Without this awareness, there would be nothing to be conscious of any experience at all. Nobody denies that some being is present in all of their experiences. The problem is that every concept of our being is as distinct from our reality as the distinction between a bridge and the blueprint of that bridge.

When we believe something that is false, that false belief exists in awareness. We simply take awareness for granted. It's almost trivial, except for the fact that we don't recognize awareness as a fact and then mistakenly identify ourselves with the thoughts and experiences that come and go in awareness. When our ideas about ourselves crumble, we might kill ourselves, try to rebuild the old identity, try to build a new identity, or become open to the possibility that there is something wrong with our concepts of who we are. If we've devoted a large part of our lives to seeking and still keep missing this problem of identification, then the experience of disillusionment feels worse because we've given so much of ourselves to spirituality and remain discontent. We begin to despair. Our lives have undoubtedly changed because of our efforts, hopefully for the better, but a disillusionment of a spiritual identity makes it seem like much of that time and effort we spent was for little or nothing. This disillusionment is implicit in the story of Buddha when he realized the failure of his efforts, even his perfect renunciation. This disillusionment is an opportunity to investigate the idea that what we call 'self' is a fiction. It is a wild ride when we begin to inquire about who we really are because it takes us into aspects of our being previously unknown or denied. It is not a common inquiry; it requires great courage, humor, passion, and more of ourselves than we ever anticipated. In self-inquiry, we are the criterion in our own lives. Don't settle for anything less than the recognition of the awareness that includes all of our human qualities and imperfections.

Awareness cannot be the same as the experiences that come and go within it. Again, when we look at our most beautiful qualities, we will see awareness shining there. When we look at our petty and cruel qualities, we also see this same awareness shining there. When we recognize that this awareness exists in all passing experience, we stop being caught in identification with experience in the same way that we don't identify the wild geese with the lake that reflects their images.

One huge advantage of not identifying ourselves with our experiences is that we have no need to regulate our faculties, such as reason, observation, and intuition, in order to sustain our self-concepts, which are as temporary as any thoughts. This recognition gives us the freedom to see a mistaken belief and not be threatened by that clarity. The understanding of right from wrong is transformed by the realization that we need not defend a sense of self that disappears in a moment of no mind, in the space between two thoughts. Awareness is big enough to hold all of our humanness; the difficult part is to recognize awareness when we habitually treat the experiences that come and go as either who we are literally or proof of who we are.

THE PARADOX

1. A statement that seems to contradict common belief, but may, nevertheless, be true

2. A self-contradictory statement or proposition

3. A person or thing that seems to possess contradictory qualities and is, thus, inexplicable or inscrutable; an enigma

Why a paradox of self-realization? Conceiving of ourselves or creating an identity is probably one of our oldest habits and the self we reference is fiction. That conceptual self occurs within us, which makes the concept a type of circular logic. Any idea of self cannot contain the self from which it arises. We witness beliefs about ourselves change throughout our lives as our circumstances, bodies, and thinking changes. I suggest that our identities are just useful mental schematics. We imagine ourselves going to the dentist and what we need to do to get there, like taking a bus or driving. What actually happens to us on our journey will be something different than what we imagined. The distance between who we are and our imagined identities is like the distance between the banana we eat and the thought of the banana. The concept of the banana does not contain any calories. Life becomes unnecessarily painful and confusing when we mistake our concept of self as real instead of as a bundle of habitual thinking. Our concept can be falsified in a thousand ways without causing us any harm.

Poetically, we can say that life dances its way into countless forms and, apparently, is lost in those forms. When we are lost in the mind, limited concepts about ourselves become the center of our identities and we must constantly battle with the events of our body-mind and environment to sustain that sense of self. Such a useless war is a waste of our life and time.

The person who mistakes who he/she is with a conceptual identity is bound in a type of vicious circle of identifying with thoughts, feelings, and/or body sensations and then feeling shocked when the events of life, like some new fact or understanding, demolish the concept of self. Spiritual seekers also suffer this identification with feeling, but in a different form, because the mistake of identification also happens with non-typical experiences. I refer to spiritual experiences that typically arise when we arrest habits of the mind in rituals or meditation. These experiences are often difficult to describe and are referred to as 'energy' or some other vague esoteric terminology, like 'Shakti' or 'chi.' Inscrutable language typically raises the eyebrows of skeptics. I suggest that we simply refer to these non-typical experiences as altered states, like drug experiences that are hard to label in everyday words. If we mistake our experiences for who we are or some proof of who we are, then those identities are threatened when the experiences pass or we encounter some aspects of ourselves that are contrary to our self-concepts. In order to feel comfortable with the inconsistencies we discover between our identities and changing facts, we must deny or rationalize away those aspects of ourselves that don't fit into our concepts of self, which is a lot of unneeded struggle and work. I'm saying that, through the recognition of awareness itself, we can be spared this struggle. Life has enough problems without fighting to sustain mind shadows as if our lives depended upon them. They don't. I suspect that it is only through awakening to awareness that we can even hope to live without denying some relevant facts about ourselves or our lives in an effort to sustain an ultimately unsustainable self. I say that we can face even the ugliest aspects of life, the worst aspects of ourselves, and feel emotions coming and going, even pain, yet remain free from a manufactured prison of identity.

A life not limited to the autopilot of our mental habits is lived within the body-mind and experience. No freedom exists from the body-mind and experience. I doubt those individuals who profess to know only the freedom of being, but deny participation in the world, such as those individuals who embrace renunciation. The freedom that I discuss here is untouched by events, so why not participate in the unfolding dance of life and embrace life in the circumstances it offers. If the teaching can't help someone do that, then I doubt its value. Self-mortification is not a virtue and is often a vain display in a quest of glory.

Life is the criterion and means of awakening. We need not change anything about ourselves to achieve awareness because awareness is already here, it is just obscured by thought. The recognition that we cannot be what comes and goes within us happens to individuals who are unpretentious, not to those individuals who are trying to be something they can never be. We change constantly regardless our self concepts, but such changes happen as adaptations to life circumstances unrestricted by our fictional identities. One reason that our concept of self changes throughout our lives is because our circumstances often show us that our ideas of ourselves are inadequate.

The unity of life is the union of (seeming) opposites. The tide comes in and the tide goes out and the ocean remains what it really is regardless of those distinctions. To be honest and accept all of the capacities that we discover in ourselves is to have a chance to account for the aspects previously hidden or stifled by our mental identities. The next challenge is to let awareness reveal itself to us in the form of other people with other ideas.

IDEOLOGIES OR MENTAL MALIGNANCIES

I will try to illuminate some points of this huge topic that are relevant to the problem of identity. When I say ideology, I mean a system of thought generally supported by some sort of political, moral, or economic motivation. This system of thought assumes a Utopian vision in a yet-to-be realized future or life beyond death. I'm not saying that making plans for the future is wrong; I'm just saying that life does not have an obligation to live up to anyone's expectations.

Someone may say that being idealistic doesn't hurt anything. I would beg to differ. Ideologies separate nations, races, and the sexes. Stalinists killed millions trying to purge undesirables from the communist society and, in the process, created a realm of deceitful conformity. Ideals have also caused people to reject aspects of their own lives when they haven't conformed to the chosen ideal. How many times have we heard someone say in a rage "I'm not angry"? They have a concept of themselves that disowns the facts. Their statement exposes either an inability or unwillingness to accept a reality. If a person can't own his or her anger, then it is doubtful that the person will account for any damage that he or she might do in anger. I'm not saying that anger is bad. Anger is a part of being human, but we must account for it. If we pretend that anger isn't there when it is, then we live in an idealistic fantasy similar to sleepwalking and there is little or no opportunity to be accountable in such a fantasy.

The more someone becomes fixated on a particular ideology, the less room there is for anything beyond the habits that attempt to sustain those beliefs. Such beliefs seem to reflect the concept of self. Some ideals become so much of a second nature to us that we forget what our lives were like without them. We don't pop into this world being progressive, conservative, or religious. Take, for example, the ideal of racial superiority. This idea is one that I am familiar with as I grew up in a redneck environment and was exposed to subtle, and, sometimes, not so subtle, ideas of this kind. If you look, then you can see that this idea is responsible for countless deaths and unfathomable misery around the world. Reality cannot be contained in any ideal regardless of how strong the belief; reality is just too large. This reality includes all of the variations of people who are themselves constantly changing. Ideologies tend to leave out much that is relevant for both changing individuals and cultures to appear more reliable. For example, it is a different thing to date someone from another race, religion, class, or caste if you come from a bigoted background. It's one example, but it shines a light on the limits of a bigoted ideology.

The whole point of any ideology is to gain something beneficial or even just the confidence that we are 'doing the right thing.' However, if we refuse to alter ideals to conform to facts, then we may be tempted to alter facts to conform to ideals. We assume a great deal when we accept an ideology. For example, we assume the superiority of our chosen ideals over others that are available and we assume that we can achieve our desired ends through these chosen ideals. We also assume that those ends are worth having. Let's go out on a limb and assume that all of the above assumptions are true, even still, anything that can be attained will be lost sooner or later; that is the price we must pay to live in a phenomenal world.

If we look to the past, then we will see that our ancestors missed the cruelty in many of their ideals. Consider the ideals pursued when Europe decided to colonize Africa, Asia, and the Americas. I refer to the 'civilizing' of native tribes considered savage. How many of these native cultures exist today? Were any of the advances that resulted worth all of the death and misery that occurred? Couldn't we have created trade and built railways without persecuting, slaughtering, and enslaving others? I ask these rhetorical questions in order to shine a light on this point. We can pay a terrible price for our ideals and they may bring failure and misery in their wake. This refusing to see the errors in an ideal is not just a collective problem, it applies to individuals as well. Often, the few who profit from the ideals accepted by a mass of followers do not live up to them personally, not by a long shot. Will our modern ideals be seen to be as backward as so many of the ideals of our ancestors seem to us today? I think it is almost a certainty. Our offspring will have the advantage of seeing the consequences of our mistakes.

What about counterculture ideals? Every counterculture that I've seen contains people who have ego trips that are not so different from the ego trips prevalent in the culture that they reject; they just deal with them differently. Some of these countercultural experiments seem better than others because they are less destructive. When we look behind the exterior, sometimes it's hard to see the difference between traditional culture and counterculture. The payoff often promised or inferred in joining a countercultural movement is supposed to be something great and, sometimes, the letdown is painful.

There is nothing wrong with using ideals in terms of trying new things. Trial and error is different from assuming the result and assuming that we would enjoy the result if people only lived up to the ideal. Identifying ourselves with ideals leads to ignoring and/or denying the results of our actions for the sake of the identity. Like the communists under Stalin who did the murderous footwork to purge all dissent in the Soviet Union, these Russian idealists tried to create an ideal society. The same kind of justification happens in relationships if we judge ourselves by our ideals and intentions; but regardless of intentions, anyone affected by our actions must reckon with the fact based consequences. Let us take the ideal of celibacy among priests and their sexual violation of children as another horrible example. The beautiful ideal of purity hid a debased, selfish, and predatory perversion that preyed upon the most vulnerable.

Ideologies are limited and limiting and, if we identify ourselves with them, then our lives become bound to those limits and any hidden falsehoods. Sooner or later, life drags us beyond the limits of our beliefs, whether we like it or not. Now, here is a twist: many ideological systems have something true in them and that's a problem. A partial truth is worse than a lie because a lie can usually be exposed. An ideal that has a segment of truth to it will always give a person something to cling to.

Consider the varying ideals in different cultures around the expectations of men and women. I personally know women who have starved themselves to fit some image of sexy. Never mind that they were sexy before this ideal distorted the fact. The criterion wasn't that they felt good or that their bodies functioned well, only the ideal mattered. This ideal definitely came from their culture. I never saw one of them live up to their own idealistic expectations, even after surgery. They either relaxed into their reality or continued to chase the ideal. Remember that there is big money in the cosmetic industry because so many have an interest in maintaining an unrealistic ideal.

Take a married couple that I know who are clinging to a relationship that is, by all appearances, dead. Most of us know people in similar circumstances. They don't have sex and no love seems to exist between them, only convenience. The price for that convenience is terribly high. For this couple, the price is a strange loyalty to the ideals on which they founded the relationship. There does not appear to be room for their broken hearts or starving sexual instincts. They both lament and feel resentment toward each other and at least one of them cheats. A lot of unnecessary anguish is going on. I am reminded of a Zen kōan that I heard a long time ago: Tie two birds together and, even though they have four wings, they cannot fly. Like the couple above, we are all exposed to popular wisdom offering ideal models for how relationships should be. Anyone might be confused by popular ideals, especially when a lot of them seem good. When we consider the results of such popular wisdom, there is much room for doubt. We pick what we think are the best ideals available and give them a try, but let's not construct our identities out of them. Those ideals can't be our identity because we can exist without them.

The relationship mistakes exemplified above have variations in other realms of our lives. We say "This is who I am…" and fill in the space with something we believe or do. Some of us might identify with our profession, but that is not who we are, that is what we do. Some of us identify with a religion or spirituality, but that isn't who we are, that is what we believe. Sometimes, after we've accepted and identified ourselves with a belief, our habits of the mind trick us. We think something like "without this belief (or identity), I can't live" and that thought is often a lie. Whether that lie involves an ideal about relationships, circumstances, or beliefs, we may have little or no reason to think it true. Our identity; our self-concept may indeed be shattered by some event and that identity may not survive the change, but identity is only a concept about ourselves. Let's look at non-sexual examples of being identified with ideals. Some people believe they're only secure as part of a religious/spiritual group. Patriotism is identification with a nation and, if we take America as a case in point, the 'freedom and justice for all' part of the allegiance pledge seems often to exclude people of color and Native Americans. The ideal and the reality are two different things.

We are more than what we think. We are also the awareness in which any thought occurs. Again, the problem is that this awareness is obscured by thoughts that seem to reinforce and prove our present identities. Our routines of thinking keep us bound in a fraction of our beneficial capacities, such as observation, reason, or intuition. Each of these aspects of cognition can act as a check on the others. When someone says "I can't live without my boyfriend or girlfriend," that may be how it feels, but, rationally, it's nonsense. Sometimes, people kill themselves or others instead of living without some particular person.

We recognize this action as delusion when people stalk media stars. We see that the stalkers don't really know the people they obsess over; therefore, the obsession must be within their own imaginations. However, why should similar imaginations be taken as more credible when they occur in people who have been together for years?

Sometimes a spouse's identity is as wrapped up in their longtime partner as the stalker's identity is centered on the unknown media star. Both might believe that they can't exist without the other and both can lead to deadly reactions. Are these ideals really so different? If we remove the identification with the 'other' in both cases, then being together or not becomes circumstantial and the apparent threat vanishes. That concept of self is not really who we are. It can die a thousand times and we will live on. The self-concept rises and falls constantly and vanishes in a moment of quiet mind; this happens throughout our lives repeatedly and we survive. We don't have the identities that we had in previous years or even yesterday. Perhaps, we should learn from our experiences.

ADDICTION

When I say 'addiction,' I mean a destructive relationship to something that is mood altering and continues regardless of life damaging or life-threatening consequences. Various forms of addiction exist and some are more visible than others. Alcoholism, drug abuse, and eating disorders are the more obvious versions. The subtler forms of addiction are what I will address. I use the word 'addiction' for lack of better. The phrase 'destructive habit' works, but does not communicate the seriousness I hope to convey. We also alter our moods with our thinking. Altering our moods becomes a destructive habit and if that habit becomes damaging, then it falls into the realm of addiction as defined above. Interpreting the world through our beliefs alters how we feel about the world. The problem is that people often don't even know when they alter their moods with thought and they treat the feelings induced as proof of a fact outside the mind, when, in reality, it is only conceptual. The fabric of our culture is shot through with such thinking.

I use addiction as one way of looking at destructive habits of the mind, including ideologies. If a person trades a life-threatening addiction, such as smoking, for another, such as an eating disorder, then it seems to be a trade up. If one needs to move from one addiction to another, hopefully, it is to a less dangerous addiction. It is a lot harder to kill yourself with food than it is with alcohol, but it can be done. I've seen addiction in rampant forms. I don't think these drugs are bad; some people simply suffer terribly as a result of using these substances.

How do we treat idealism that is maladapted to our lives, especially if that idealism is popular? If your system of thought is in accord with the popular wisdom of the day, then, when you become disillusioned, everyone will feel sorry for you. If you begin to seek alternatives, then they will say that you've become a gullible dupe of another system of thought. I remember some of my adolescent friends accusing me of being brainwashed after I stopped using drugs. I couldn't convince them that I hadn't found any life affirmation in trying to constantly stay high. I ended up leaving most of those people behind. They felt that I had betrayed our shared way of life, and I had. This type of reactivity is the same when someone leaves an idealistic fold. It may be a conventional mindset, such as Christianity; a spiritual community; or a country. Some of those individuals left behind feel betrayed and threatened.

Let's now consider the person who is separating himself/herself from some ideology. The pain that the body-mind goes through in disillusionment is not unlike the psychological pain that a drug addict feels when he runs out of dope. Disillusionment is not uncommon because facts can blatantly falsify what we think. Have you ever bounced a check because you didn't pay attention to the balance in your account? The phrase 'ignorance is bliss' comes to mind. When the truth is revealed, then there is disillusionment. We are forced from our fictitious world of thought and enter the quite different reality of bank charges when this situation occurs. Such a shock is indicative, although much less intense, of what happens when a person experiences a disillusionment with his identity. When a belief about who we are is shattered, then we feel that life is desolate. In order to avoid this feeling, we surround ourselves with like-minded people and feed our addictions to beliefs like a tweeker at the dope man's house. We probably won't die of belief withdrawals, like an alcoholic might when his body suffers delirium tremens. However, we may have a nervous breakdown or become suicidal when our beliefs fail. Sometimes, people are so quick to explain away contradictions or pick up new beliefs that they hardly have a chance to live even a few moments without the burden of beliefs obscuring the reality of the unknown.

Let's digress to remember a distinction between belief and awareness. Some fact or reason might convince us that some new belief is truer. This new recognition threatens our previous beliefs. Awareness can't be threatened because it's present in both the old and new beliefs, regardless of which is better. A person who has never turned inward in meditation will probably doubt this statement about awareness, but it is not difficult to grasp. A person who has never tasted chocolate may read about chocolate and how to prepare chocolate dishes, but, if he hasn't actually tasted chocolate, then he doesn't know what it tastes like, even if everyone says it is good. Once you have tasted double chocolate cake, you know what all of the fuss is about as the tasting brings about understanding. Awareness is subjective and a skeptic is right to say that the above example is weak. The analogy essentially says that "if you knew the truth, then you would agree," but such illustrations help us to understand that, sometimes, the taste of truth can shatter beliefs and that is something that any skeptic can appreciate. Some people let their children die because they don't believe in medicine. Instead, they believe that a god will heal their children. When the children die, that is a powerful disillusionment. I remember one instance where one parent chose to believe that it was God's will that the child became sick, while the other parent began to question their system of belief after the child died. It's hard for me to comprehend a belief that could remain after such a falsification, but, when we have identified ourselves with a belief or have some other vested interest, we desire to explain away results contrary to the belief.

If we accidentally put our hands on a hot stove and burn ourselves, then we have a direct experience. If people tell us that a hot stove is safe to touch, then we say boldly that they are mistaken and we probably won't be manipulated, even if thousands of people disagree with us. However, if identity is involved, then we feel tempted to doubt even our own experiences.

Someone may argue that he or she doesn't credit any system of thought any more than the public facts suggest and, therefore, may be able to avoid thought systems ending in the word 'ism.' Assuming that is true, I would still insist that a probing discussion about systems of thought and identity is still relevant to anyone with a mind because people build world views out of how they habitually think about themselves. Identity is a system of thought. For example, women have a reason, occasionally, to complain about the insensitivity of men. Some women, and many men, build identities that exclude their more emotional aspects. Some people mistake emotion for weakness and treat a lack of emotion as strength. Granted, some situations exist where emotionalism will sabotage one's intentions. If we wake to find our house is on fire, then we can't afford to become overwhelmed emotionally. I suggest that our capacity to disobey emotion is useful, like a tool. However, like all tools, when the job is done, you don't take the tool into other areas of your life. Imagine a logger who dresses up to go out to dinner with his beloved. He takes her hand in his left and his chainsaw in his right and enters the restaurant. The example is absurd, but when someone builds an identity around being unemotional, we see an analogous display. An emergency room surgeon facing traumatic injuries may need to somehow sidestep the horror of what he or she sees in order to help. If the surgeon collapses or is delayed by emotional upheaval, then he or she becomes less helpful, which defeats his or her purpose. That surgeon can still have access to those emotions, but if he or she identifies himself or herself as being unfeeling in order to maintain that identity, then he or she would probably feel a need to deny the emotion, even when alone.

We tend to build a system of thought about ourselves, a schematic that excludes other aspects of who we are for the sake of sustaining the preferred identity. Is this habit of exclusion so much different than someone turning away from facts that disagree with his ideological system? I don't think so. Let's be more specific. Some people identify themselves with anger, which, then, becomes the dominant center of their world views. Anger gets mistaken for strength. I tell such people that they don't lose the ability to be angry when exploring any other viewpoint of which they are capable, for example viewing any situation with compassion. The relief in some of these people is so evident that you can see their bodies relax. They believed that to dare step outside of their anger would leave them defenseless.

The habit of identity involves exclusion, which is why an innate fear exists of discovering anything new about ourselves. The mind is too small to contain all of who we are. Mental events have a beginning; therefore, they have an end and that includes the concept of self. The mind tries to exclude or explain away relevant things for the sake of certainty. These mental gymnastics are unnecessary and a source of great suffering. The mind occurs in awareness, like the weather changing in the vast sky, the sky represents awareness. The weather, be it sunshine or a storm, represents mind. Much of who we are has nothing to do with the mind in all its genius and folly. If we find every one of our concepts listed alphabetically in a dictionary, then how many are original? These concepts are what we build our identities around and we have simply absorbed them secondhand. Let's look at these concepts as tools, not as who we are. Even spiritual seekers who grasp the problem of identity probably refer to a secondhand idea of enlightenment. They turn their ideas about freedom into a reflection or proof of their current identities, only, now, they think of themselves as enlightened or un-enlightened beings based on their preconceived enlightenment ideals.

Identity is just a mental stand-in for ourselves when we conceive of the world and ourselves in it. It is not real. We need not defend our identities because what is not real need not be defended. Once we have unburdened ourselves of treating fiction as reality, we may feel at odds with others. Authority figures tell us what is good and bad and, clearly, they often do not agree among themselves. People who previously wielded power over us lose their power because they cannot threaten us by threatening our fictional identities. We will also be at odds with others because we won't believe that any ideological system of belief represents who we or they are. It's better to deal with the difficulties of seeing our mental constructs and their faults and limitations than to suffer the pain of trying to pretend those faults and limits don't exist. Let's not waste our time asking ideas to be more than what they are or pretending to be something that we are not.

The good news is that the recognition of awareness, regardless of any self-concept, takes us deeper into the discovery of life because no ideology or identity will separate us from the choices that life might offer. If we are trying to be something that we aren't, then there is no possibility of this realization of awareness itself and we become bound in concepts about ourselves. It seems that a person becomes willing to be more of who he or she is only after trying a limited identity and finding it lacking. We can always find or create other identities and there are countless forces pulling us to do so.

A prominent notion exists that, if we could successfully control our environments, then we would be happy. For example, someone may believe that, if only my boyfriend/girlfriend weren't such an asshole, things would be good. If only I had a better job or more money, then things would be good. If only I were better looking, then I would be OK. If only people would just listen to or do what I say, then they would see my good intentions. Spirituality has its own variation on this theme: If I could just surrender more, trust more, have faith, be a good practitioner, be more disciplined, and meditate three hours a day, then I would be happy or could sustain happiness (or peace or whatever the ideal is). The list goes on and on. We see that any benefits often exist in the mind as an imagined future. This emotionally charged imagination gives us both a diversion and an identity with being a seeker. Given agreeable circumstances, such as having money, property, and prestige, a seeker may not have an impulse to consider anything else because the seeking is ego gratifying and appears to be able to sustain the concept of self, which is an illusion. It is when disillusionment occurs that we open ourselves up to something else, usually just long enough to build a new identity based on another belief system.

SPIRITUAL POLITICS

Politics are a pain in the ass; the chicanery, butt kissing, and Machiavellian rationalizing seem agitating at best and malevolent at worst. I wish to avoid participating in such matters, much like trying to avoid stepping in dog shit. Still, there are times when we discover it on our shoes (that smell lets us know); then, we must deal with the consequences that follow.

Spiritual politics are no less rank than ordinary politics. Anyone who has been involved seriously with spiritual movements will probably understand what I am saying. I once heard a teacher try to excuse his own cunning bullshit by saying that all communication is political, meaning that, in any relationship, we are always mired in some kind of pecking order and usury. We can try to avoid the bog of politics by clearly stating our intentions and letting others make up their minds. Motives simply spoken work against a political agenda as they give others something to oppose. I am comfortable with such opposition and it's a small price to pay for a way out of the bog.

An awakened life is a life lived without being blinded by concepts of ourselves. There are certainly a lot of different teachings in the world. I will not say that I am the alpha and omega of awakening. Teachers who say that their teachings are the only way are being political; it is just that simple. If one is discontent, then check out other authors or teachers. If you find something that serves you, then great. I am critical of other teachings and they should be so with me. I leave the door open for a few reasons, not because I like what others teach, but because a group of people in a closed system breed a herd mentality, a collective mind. In those types of systems, no one person's thinking or actions can go beyond the group's thinking or actions without experiencing consequences from that group. Typically, an individual's statements are not allowed to question, challenge, or surpass those teachings and statements made by the authority figure, be it a guru or professional helper. In a group, such 'arrogance' has a tendency to piss everyone off, especially the guru or leader. Such close-mindedness is dogma, pure and simple, and, in a group, it becomes institutionalized and stagnant.

Progress exists because our ancestors were willing to exchange older beliefs for better beliefs. There is something terrifying about a step of progress that changes the way we look at the world and that terror holds us back collectively (and individually). Any new discovery, spiritual or otherwise, often meets resistance from existing tradition. There was a time when it appeared certain that man would never fly. American newspapers did not report the Wright brothers' test flight at Kitty Hawk for this reason.

I'm not saying that collective groups are not worthwhile. Great discoveries take place as a result of people trying to achieve a common goal, but a collective mind where people think alike can also be terribly destructive and utterly insane. The Heaven's Gate cult is proof enough of that. The system was closed and isolated and the collective mind ended in genital mutilation and mass suicide. It seems that denial and credulity are two enemies that continue to haunt human progress. A collective mind is a powerful and dangerous thing.

Zen Buddhists have a name for being trapped in a particular system of thought or teaching: "dharma ridden." A person becomes so attached (identified) to a particular teacher or teaching that he renders the teaching ineffective as a result. The teaching becomes important as a badge of prestige or self-satisfaction. The result is spiritual pride. During my time as a seeker, I wrestled with this issue. It is a subtle and powerful realm of mental habit. When we identify ourselves with a system of thought and strive to obey the ideology, we blind ourselves to good things, possibilities that exist outside of that ideology. Even assuming that we possess a valuable understanding of ourselves and others, change still happens and we would be foolish to say "our world-view is the only one that works" because, even if it were true, the next moment, it may not be true.

Any subjective understanding demonstrates integrity by helping people accept and adapt to the actual circumstances of their lives. For example, the recognition that we need not bind ourselves to any habitual way we conceive of ourselves, shows that we can not only think of ourselves outside of those same habits, we can adapt ourselves outside those habits. This recognition gives us a better understanding of our minds. It's like we have awaken from a dream. Such an awakening shows us that our imaginations cause reality loss when we treat concepts as facts, particularly concepts about ourselves. If a teaching helps people awaken, then why would that teaching close the system? I have heard many reasons for closing a spiritual society from outside influences. The most often used one is because people may be confused by different expressions and, thus, won't be able to concentrate all of their energy and attention on what is being offered in that particular group. This reason doesn't go far enough. It is a symptom of the collective mind, which typically dismisses other beliefs as ignorant and separates itself from critics. This arrogance of the system is typified by the attempt to hide the fact that elitism actually exists by accusing others of arrogance. For example, read the contemptuous indictment against Galileo, whose crimes amounted to telling and proving the truth. The Catholic inquisitors felt so sure of themselves and their unquestionable wisdom that they persecuted one of the greatest minds of their time.

A teaching involving subjective inquiry cannot offer proof, like poor Galileo and his telescope, so we have more reason to question what people call wisdom in any subjective realm. A subjective teaching must point out its unique offerings in order to attract those individuals who might need or want what it has to offer. The same is true of political parties, colleges, or restaurants; it's called marketing. One of the things that I appreciate about schools of martial arts is that, despite faulting other schools, they will face other schools in tournaments and talk is cheap. In the fighting ring, you have a chance to demonstrate your competence or incompetence; whatever happens, you will learn something from your opponent. The result is often humility.

The individual who approaches a teacher who deals with subjective experience must discern between what is helpful and what is harmful, but, when a teaching itself is the criterion, then the scrutiny becomes almost useless. A direct contradiction of the teacher or doctrine will, at least, raise an eyebrow. Who the hell is the seeker to question the authority of the teacher, therapist, or priest? For example, if a teacher says "Do X and Y will happen" and instead Z happens, then what is the honest student to do? These contradictions are typical when dealing with subjective methods of self inquiry. As such, it's easy to excuse them through an interpretation of the teaching itself or explain them away as a fault of the student. Here, we have the recipe for religious apologists explaining away the worst of deceptions and human behavior. The critical thinking required to see such a fault isn't well-developed in much of society. I suggest that, if one is interested in a subjective inquiry, then one must expose oneself to criticisms and different teachings in order to discover whether one's teachings actually reveal harmless benefits in harmony with facts. Unfortunately, no simple way exists to prove subjective competence. Take psychiatry as an example. The authority that labeled homosexuality as a mental illness was not so different from the authority that declared the opposite in 1973.

"The evolution of the status of homosexuality in the classifications of mental disorders highlights that concepts of mental disorder can be rapidly evolving social constructs that change as society changes."

Let's look at problems in spiritual groups. A seeker may need to separate from a school that or teacher who helped him in real ways. It may be because the seeker finds fault or outgrows the teaching. It may be that the seeker cannot really participate or is unhappy. Perhaps the student is limited by his or her own prejudice, but it might also be the prejudices or arbitrary limits of the group. In such cases, it need not be a problem if the group is open and the seeker can come and go and return as the case may be. When the system is closed, which may be a matter of degree, outside ideas and scrutiny become taboo. It is tumultuous and sad that, in order to follow an impulse, perhaps toward something truer, one may need to separate from others who are holding him or her back. Imagine yourself in this position. When leaving a closed system, you will probably need to separate yourself from those individuals who are still involved in it, especially if the group or teacher perceives you as a political threat or competition. (After all, if what a particular school offers is the best that one can hope for, then why would anyone ever leave?) It is common for teachers and followers left behind to personally attack those individuals who leave, attempting to strip them of credibility. A subtler form of character assassination is to see those individuals who have left as wounded, broken, or otherwise unable to live the 'truth' of the teaching. In this case, the attack looks compassionate. Others involved know the same will happen to them if they leave; it is like cauterizing a wound to get it to stop bleeding. Our vanity about what other people think becomes a weapon against us. Political and religious groups use the same tactics. Sadly, when people leave, a sense of betrayal is felt by all. People in this position are leaving friends, lovers, and support that they have known, perhaps, for years and this loss is compounded by the grief of separation from a trusted authority figure, guru, or teacher.

If we won't accept our autonomy, then our fates will always be relative to the will of the group or teacher and that is not being personally responsible. It's possible that, for some people, being absorbed into a group might be the best thing that they could have ever hoped to achieve. For others, it is a hell because they feel that they can't survive without the group or teacher. They are prisoners bound by dependence. Not knowing what else to do, they become like people trapped in a bad marriage. If and when these people leave, it often happens with great resentment. Once opposing sides are taken, individuals on either side of the separation might even try, in their anger and hurt, to harm those individuals seen as opponents. I have seen this situation more than once.

As a young man, I involved myself in groups with a therapist named Alex. The cathartic emotional work that he led felt awesome to participate in and behold. I was 18 at the time and benefited from the experience. The groups became larger and Alex's prestige grew. Therapists trained under Alex and, fortunately, I participated in these training groups since, at that time, I worked as a counselor in the field of addiction recovery. Alex became a kind of teacher/father figure by default. The techniques provoked emotional catharsis that few involved had ever seen. Many of the people working with Alex wanted to be near him and began to work for him for that reason. One of these people was a woman named Barbara. The second time she came to see Alex, she asked him if he wanted to fuck. Alex refused and everyone knew the story because Barbara herself joked about it. The therapy itself involved a lot of physical contact. It was not uncommon to touch a person on the heart when they wept. The contact was harmless. About three years passed and Barbara, acting like a spurned lover, got together with two other therapists, a husband and wife team, who worked and trained under Alex, and accused him of sexual harassment, hoping for financial gain and to slander Alex to clients. In the end, they stole clients. Alex did indeed place his hand on Barbara's heart, over her breasts, and he was her boss. These actions led to Alex being disgraced publicly. He felt betrayed. Barbara gave the same physical contact to her clients, but that made no difference.

Years later, Barbara and her cohorts attempted to make amends with Alex for their lies and wrongdoing. Alex responded by saying that he would accept their apology only if they contacted everyone they had lied to and apologized to them as well. They refused. I, by chance, began working as a counselor with Barbara in an inpatient treatment center for addictions. The whole time I worked there, she never looked me in the eyes or spoke a word of our past. Barbara and I were friends for about three years before this whole event took place.

Moving from therapy back to spiritual teachers and gurus, I know that there are a few out there who discuss inquiry into the conscious nature, what I refer to as awareness. To be in the presence of one who recognizes this awareness is good fortune, although he or she may communicate that realization differently. I spoke with a man, at a public gathering, who happened to be acquainted with a teacher (guru) from whom I had separated. I asked this man a simple question regarding a difficulty he felt in sexual relationships. The question was this: "Have you come this far (meaning the difficulties he had gone through finding his sexuality) to be deprived?" He felt distant and sexually cut off from his lover and there was no sense, at that time, that the circumstances would change. The question, apparently, helped him clarify where he stood. A woman present reported this conversation to my old teacher, suggesting that I was some sort of threat to his school. The teacher got angry and proceeded to personally and publicly attack me. He stated that he would need to purify this man I had spoken to (by performing an exorcism, I guess) in order to protect this man from my harmful influence. I didn't like this insult. The fact that what I said helped him to clarify what he wanted meant nothing to this teacher. He feared losing people to me, perceived me as a political threat, and wanted to put a stop to that threat. He even presumed to suggest that, if I attended any events with "his" people present, I should remain silent. Frankly, I got angry. I had done nothing wrong. The man I helped had been a friend for years prior to his relationship with this guru. To demonize me seemed absurd and, most of the people present when I spoke, knew this fact. People spoke up and, eventually, this teacher apologized to me, which I appreciated. The apology was politically motivated, which took away from its authenticity. When this guru slandered me, it was to his advantage politically and, when his crowd began to see that he was in the wrong, he apologized. It was also to his advantage politically. I took his apology as a token gesture. It was better than a stick in the eye and I knew that it was all that I would get. I felt no desire to end up in a conflict with a man who had, at one time, helped me. I made it clear, though, that I would not tolerate his lies.

The above is an example of spiritual politics and it stinks. Another example can be found in a yoga temple where I once lived. Before I relate this story, I want to mention that I possess a strong intuition, although I will admit that I've been wrong. However, in general, I tend to be correct when it comes to people. My intuition is subtle, almost like whispering, and I've felt skeptical about it myself. For example, at 19, my roommate and I lived in an apartment complex. I repeatedly expressed a bad feeling about our upstairs neighbor. My roommate, who thought me eccentric, suggested that I was paranoid since we never actually had any bad experiences with this young man. Later, our neighbor shot a man in anger in front of our door. We literally stepped over the blood. I did point out to my roommate that he was wrong about my intuition, knowing fully that I could never prove this statement as a fact. An intuition (a guess) is essentially a sensitivity to feeling what is going on in another person's inner world. It is not reading people. It is feeling people. Sometimes, what I feel appears to be contrary to what a particular person is presenting publicly. I have something of a reputation for speaking what I sense.

Now, for the story. I once lived on a property that was part of the yoga temple mentioned above. The woman who owned the property made it a temple and the guru readily accepted. I knew this woman for about seven years in relation to various other spiritual groups, therapists, and gurus. She had been kind to me in many ways in spite of her blind spots about her spiritual identity and love of power. She possessed a type of clarity that impressed many people. All this considered, I never trusted her. This woman, prominent in the temple, was recognized as being fully awakened and an enlightened adept of spiritual transmission meaning she was capable of sharing her understanding with others She was called "the queen of down" because she was said to inhabit the dark, emotional places where others would not dare to go. People bowed to her and touched her feet when they saw her, a gesture of respect from the guru tradition. They trusted her with their self inquiry. I sensed a problem. She would present herself as having great tenderness and humility around the progenitor of the temple. However, when he was not present, she would insist on dominating others in such a fashion that they couldn't trust themselves. With the sanction of the guru and the prestige of being awakened, she directed people to give up their own inquiries for the ones that she suggested. It seemed remarkable how the inquiry that she suggested always had her as a matriarch.

I mentioned to a few disbelieving people that, one day, she would dump this teacher when he no longer served her spiritual prestige. You see, this woman possessed a coercive power of suggestion. This power operated whether she knew something or not. She was such a bitch that she couldn't attract people on whom to act out her power trip. She needed somebody attractive to supply the people. I saw her do this trip with five gurus and one therapist. She disapproved of me for not showing her respect. The people involved in the temple tried to convince me, saying that I was stubborn, hyper-masculine, and chauvinistic. This defect in my personality explained why I didn't see her for "who she truly was."

I observed the effect that she had on people and wasn't buying it. She subordinated others on spiritual grounds. I questioned my feelings and asked myself if I was being unfair, but I couldn't reconcile how I felt with what I saw. I also couldn't abandon my own reasoning just to have the approval of the group and the guru. I tried to confront this situation twice. Once, I tried to arrange a meeting with the guru and some of the people involved for the purpose of confronting this woman and holding her accountable for her actions. She convinced the teacher that the meeting wasn't necessary. Another time, she said something to me that was not only presumptuous and wrong, but utterly contradicted the guru's teachings. I made her repeat herself several times so that I could be sure of what I heard, then, I confronted her in a group setting in the presence of the teacher. Speaking out felt uncomfortable for me. She simply denied the facts and stated that I must have misunderstood her. I knew then that I could not address her power trip without hard evidence. Frankly, she had her nose so far up the teacher's ass that he couldn't imagine her being anything, but benign. His gratitude for her generosity blinded him and he couldn't see her clearly until her arrogance couldn't be denied.

Within two months, the woman above threw the guru and all of his gifts to her out. She insisted that he give back all of the gifts that she had given him. Then, she proceeded to publicly attack his character with both real and imagined faults. I ended up being the last to leave the property and dealt with this woman after she revealed her true colors. She couldn't receive even a fraction of the criticism she had dished out. The point of the story is that a profound inquiry requires responsibility and integrity and such traits are not as common as one might think. The willingness to change our minds when life or someone else gives us a good reason to doubt beliefs is the mark of integrity. Anyone can repeat a teaching like a parrot and receive respect from the mediocre who follow like lemmings, but let's not settle for that. We need courage and doubt and those qualities are the ones that all authoritarians (even the cuddly ones) fear.

If you feel interested or attracted to what I say and feel that I have something valuable to share, that's great. If you don't feel that I am giving you something valuable, then find someone who does. All I ask is that you base your judgment on investigation and not prejudice. This freedom of choice to come and go and find one's own value is basically the same orientation that I have with my lovers. If my lovers want to be with someone else, then I make room for that. I am willing to embrace the unknown so that they have access to all that life offers them. After all, they are going to be dead a long time, as am I.

SPIRITUAL BULLSHIT

I must say that this chapter has a more passionate flare to it than the previous ones. I won't cram my contempt into a tamer expression. Something that continually amazes me is the amount of spiritual crap that is served up as sustenance by so-called authorities. These people serve to continue the delusion of others. It is time to expose some of the methods that these con artists use with the hope that people will see this type of shit for what it is.

A demagogue is a person who ignites the passions of others by using very emotional language and energy. Generally, there needs to be an element of truth to what the speaker is saying or, at least, popular interest among the crowd for the subject, and the more disturbing that truth is, the better. This piece of truth is spoken into a space where others will surely agree with it. It may even be self-evident. There are certainly a lot of shocking truths and nothing wrong with speaking them as one of the ways people help one another. It is the next part of the mechanism that begins to enslave the unaware. Once an emotional truth is spoken, a truth that most people wouldn't have spoken, there is an opening of trust in the listeners. The expectation that is created is simply this: The next thing this person says will be true because the last thing he or she dared to say was obviously true. In that opening, the presumed authority has an opportunity to speculate or say anything. The half-truth or untruth simply rides upon the coattails of the truth into the mind of the listener, often going unnoticed. In such a case, what is said usually serves the speaker or his or her ideology and often exists at the listener's expense.

The rhetoric that I discuss above is an old game. We have seen it many times in political arenas and a pundit's job is to speculate using a particular ideology as a guide. I am not suggesting that all speculation is useless. I am saying that it is necessary to admit when we are speculating. Sliding from the facts to a conclusion about the facts through some flawed or dubious belief or bias causes people terrible wounds. Think of the facts like vegetables, the speculation is like cooking, and the conclusion is like soup. The facts can be true, but speculation about the facts can lead to a worthless conclusion where the facts lose all value. Just like when exceptionally good vegetables are ruined through a mistake in cooking, producing horrible soup. That's no fault of the veggies. Here is an example from religion. Most of us have been to a sermon where the priest, rabbi, or other 'authority' at some point shocks the crowd by reading an alarming story from a newspaper, like a terrible crime or natural disaster. The heads in the audience shake with disapproval and disbelief and the sound of murmuring rises from the crowd like smoke. The fact referenced by the speaker is something everyone present will likely feel emotional about and, in that emotional opening, the speaker will propose some solution to the problem. In such a situation, people want to console the horror in their bodies like a child wants his or her mother's hug after a bad dream or bee sting. People begin nodding their heads and accepting solutions simply because they don't want to be left with the pain and uncertainty of the terrible event referred to in the story. If the solution is a thesis (and it usually is), then it probably won't be able to be tested in the lives of the listeners. It will need to be taken on faith and the agreement of the crowd makes it easy to follow it. It is important to note that the solution generally aggrandizes the organization or person presenting it. Again, many of these theories fall apart the minute you look at them.

In the world of esoteric spirituality, the same mechanism works on subtler levels. I spoke in the previous chapter of a woman acting as an authority. She stunned people with her clarity and, then, insisted that they were somehow deficient or defective because they couldn't see what she did. She did not help people stand on their own feet. Instead, she tried to make them dependent on her by pointing out their flaws, both real and imagined. She didn't bother to tell these credulous seekers at what point she went beyond simply reporting the facts (as she saw them) to conjecturing about how these people ought to be. A huge difference exists between seeing something that is true in experience and inferring what should be true. Most of us notice when something like this kind of inference is happening because it feels weird, even though we may not be able to identify the fallacy. Let's call this feeling the bullshit-o-meter. We need to listen to this intuition so that we can scrutinize what we hear. Clearly, the intuition may be wrong, too. On one hand, it's possible that we are hearing something that goes against a prejudice and our discomfort springs from facing new and disagreeable facts. However, the feeling could stem from someone taking advantage of our trust. If we feel unsure, we are always free to insist that something doesn't seem right and requires further examination. If someone insists that we don't trust enough or don't have enough faith, then we still possess the freedom to disagree and put what any authority says to the best test we can create. Such trial and error takes being responsible for our own inquiries. I would bet that, if we are not responsible in this way, then we have probably found someone who will take responsibility for us, perhaps one of these demagogues.

Therapy is not beyond scrutiny either. I met a female therapist at a seminar on Maui. Her lover accompanied her and their emotional struggles struck me as more or less like any typical, American couple. She made a point of saying that she made $6,000 at a seminar for her discussion on communication with teenagers. I asked if the techniques she wrote about helped her with her own teens and, after beating around the bush, she said no. She considered her seminar worthwhile not because it helped her in her relations with her own teens but because what she offered was consistent with her learning and credentials. She is certainly not alone in this dubious professional attitude and it's astonishing that her failures with her own children did not expose the weakness to her. Consistency in a thesis, not results, becomes the acceptable standard for many professionals who work in the subjective realm. However, we should ask whether the thesis can be adapted to the real circumstances of life. If not, we should look for something better. I suggest that there is a whole lot more trial and error going on than most people are willing to admit. Regardless of intention, consistency with the popular wisdom of the day leaves a great deal of room for doubt in terms of real help that's adapted to real life in particular circumstances.

The great advantage about truth, with few exceptions, is that it is not contradicted by facts. Sometimes, it is necessary to separate the bullshit from what we actually recognize as true. After all, there is nothing worth saying that can't be said poorly. If the truth doesn't stand on its own without a bunch of rationalizations to hold it up, then I say that we have reason to doubt it. We can imagine that we are eating great delicacies, but imaginary food won't nourish us. This imagination is what I call the realm of spiritual make-believe. If someone tells me that a June bug can pull a freight train, then I say let's get a rope and hook the little bastard up and see.

Just because someone possesses some charisma or writes books doesn't mean that he or she is liberated, awakened, or self-aware. There are magicians, psychics, and energy workers who can do some inexplicable things. That doesn't mean that we should govern our lives by their advice. The only way to tell what is true from what is false in the realm of the subjective is to inquire into your own being without rejecting any of your faculties, while also fully embracing reason, observation, and intuition, particularly regarding predictions. Each faculty acts as a check on the others, seeking out errors. No aspect of our being guarantees truth, especially a subjective truth, but our faculties can expose an error by giving us real reasons to doubt. Again, the desire for truth is the only thing worthy of the term 'sacred' and exposing errors cannot be separated from that desire to discover what is true.

If we are unable to trust ourselves, then I suggest that we inquire why. Maybe we feel flawed or are afraid of making mistakes. However, making mistakes and being honest enough to admit them are a part of living, a part of integrity. Perhaps we have had more success listening to others than trusting our faculties and sensibilities. If we keep handing the responsibility of our lives to others, then we won't be able to develop the ability to be responsible for ourselves. Probably any person we rely upon feels ego gratification from the relationship. They won't lead us to our own awareness because we are subordinate to them and they like it.

SEX LIFE

Much of what follows deals with sexuality. I take the subject head on because, so much we read, hear, and see about sex is either sex as a means to an end or approached with an avalanche of rituals or idealistic thinking. Many teachers who simply create spaces where people can experience more of their capacities, which is a wonderful thing, if we remember that our capacities are inherent. If a therapist or sex guru creates a space where you can benignly delight in sexuality that you'd never imagined previously, then that guru did not give you the capacity, but, instead, created the space in which that capacity could be realized.

Sex comes and goes in awareness like any other experience, but one of the gifts of sexuality is that, at the peak of joy, we let go of our imagined selves. Ironically, sex is one of the big three subjects in which we attempt to anchor our identities. Sex, money, and death represent the events most likely to be used as props for a fictional identity. Having or not having sex, having or not having money, and how we conceive death seem to be some type of proof of who we are. This identification is a mistake because we limit our present capacities according to concepts. Whether we see our circumstances as good or bad, all circumstances change and even the richest people die. Money and lovers come and go and our identities will always remain fiction.

It's curious how we use the term 'sex life,' as in 'How is your sex life?' or 'I have no sex life,' maybe even 'We have a wonderful sex life.' It should be trivial to say that sex and life are linked because sex is the source of life. I've noticed that, in the media's portrayal of sex, it is synonymous with death or the fear of death. If you go to a horror movie, you will notice that the people who engage in sexual activity, generally, die horribly. In dramas, sex often leads to great risks in life. In films such as 9 1/2 Weeks or Indecent Proposal, the sexual pathos is emphasized. Sex is powerful, exciting, sacred, scary, painful, and fun...I love it.

Some people open up and share with me in great detail about their sex lives. This situation occasionally happens with strangers, too. I can't articulate exactly why some women open up to me in this way, but my guess is that some women know intuitively that I won't punish or shame them for being sexual. Much of what has been talked about in these conversations has been the pain of shame, deprivation, and restraint. My strong interest in sex used to put a lot of women on 'horny guy alert,' so vulnerability on their parts was generally not the norm. I don't feel any less horny than I used to; in fact, I am probably more sexual than I have ever been, but there is also a freedom that exists now that didn't in the past because I don't measure who or what I am by whether I'm having sex. I like sexual pleasure, but sex is not a requirement for me to value affection with a woman or for me to value her sexual joy when I am not the beneficiary of that joy. I simply think the world is a better place when people have access to joy.

Perhaps my sexual philosophy resonates with some people and, for that reason, it acts like an invitation to talk openly. This sexual inquiry is usually pretty simple: What is this body capable of? That question covers a lot of ground because we are all capable of multi-dimensional, creative, sexual play. What do I really need to do to respond to the facts around me? That is a more difficult question. It requires accountability for oneself and to others, if we answer it honestly.

This consideration doesn't exclude men and I don't mean to give the impression that I am supporting some radical feminist ideology when I generalize about men. I am not. I am a man and I love being a man. I want women to be as free as men and I want men to be freer. This philosophy means being able to adapt to life beyond being limited to popular beliefs. I want feminism to succeed in bringing real justice to women, which is why I criticize some feminist standards of judging evidence. I also feel that men overtly or covertly oppose women's sexual freedom because it scares men; however, women are also guilty of this rejection of female sexuality. Slut-shaming from women can be vicious, regardless of whether the one shaming indulges in the same conduct. It happens that, in my culture, men have more permission to be sexual than women. Not that men don't experience disapproval, and some of the censure is quite justified, but men are not held to the same standards as women in terms of sexual conduct. I have noticed that a large percentage of the men that I've met (I've led hundreds of men's groups.) will have affairs and rationalize these affairs. When I ask these cheating men if it would be okay if their wives took other lovers, the answer was almost always emphatically "NO!" The double standard is obvious. Women also participate in this two-faced conduct, so the principles involved are not limited to a particular gender. However, the social element of slut-shaming is its own double standard. I tend to focus on men, but will give one exception, of a woman imposing double standard. One long-term couple joined a group called 'love without limits.' The woman in this story demanded that her relationships be closed on the part of her lovers while she was free to be with both men and women. This agreement sure seemed like a limit to me, but that was the only way she would participate. She and two men agreed to these rules and even got tattoos signifying their love. The two men involved felt bitterness about their arbitrary limits and their affections deteriorated over time, although the cause of that break up we can't really say.

The truth poetically spoken is that most of us have the blood of mutilated sexuality on our hands. We have more or less accepted the arbitrary constraints and opinions of our culture or counterculture. Something that my beloved Sharon said with contempt in a group of women: "It's as if the best we [women] should get to hope for is to have one little man and we pray that he doesn't cheat on us." She related that many of the women rejected the notion when stated plainly and applauded her for saying it. They all felt that this idea seemed cruel and limiting; however, they did not change anything to get out of the limitation. The inability to realize desires has a lot to do with fear, pain, and the disillusionment that comes when society punishes people for being sexually wild, alive, and filled with joy. They have words for women like that, including 'slut' and 'whore.' These distasteful epithets are thrown around regardless of whether the sex is harmless (e.g., no violence, coercion, recklessness, deceit) and, sometimes, women receive insults just for having an unsatisfied longing or for how they dress.

If women are capable of more sexuality than they are living, then why not let them live it? For human beings the price of rejecting some or all of the sexual imperatives seems quite high. We need only look to the religious who impose strict rules and then scandalize themselves when they break those rules. We have all probably seen bad examples of common sexual beliefs, whether we refer to the failures of abstinence only education or the horrible abuses of pretentiously celibate priests. The body doesn't stop needing just because we insist otherwise; the need goes underground and operates in the fearful shadows. Fear threatens identity and, if you don't know that identity is not who you are, then you probably can't view others except in relation to that fictional identity. Fear causes people to contract and accept limitations. These limitations may be anything, but safe. They may often involve deceit. When a wife or husband bursts into a room and the partner is cheating, then the truth is known. They stand without a lie to protect them. If you aren't willing to stand in your sexuality without a lie, then the sexuality that I support is not for you. Sexual hypocrisy is a monstrous pretension and it robs others of their informed choices. Such two-faced sexuality is common. One 60-year-old man commented: "If I don't lie to women, then they won't fuck me." My experience proves that his belief is false. He is guilty of a hasty generalization. Obviously, the truth has no obligation to fulfill our desires. People who value the spoken truth may not be easy to find, but they exist. If we won't speak the truth for fear that we will miss an opportunity, then any prospective partners may never get a chance to choose from the real alternatives we offer. Since a lie robs people of their choices, including the lie of omission, lies are contrary to any understanding of freedom. Freedom without access to choices is a neutered, empty concept.

The question I ask is "Is all the suffering and dishonesty around sexuality really necessary?" I don't think so. I have a choice: I can suffer the pain of denying my reality or I can embrace and adapt to the facts, including joys and pains, as best I can. I go into problem-solving when facing real difficulties. I choose to pursue and feel the truth of my reality regardless of whether I am getting what I would like. The idea that freedom frees you from pain is simply wrong, but conscious choice based on what is actually happening is far better than a deceitful response caused by self-centered fear.

Freedom gives us access to more choices and, regardless of pleasure or pain, we are not bound to choices based on fictional identities. Pain still sucks, but it is not the boundless, futile misery of trying to sustain what isn't real. The concept of self is a virtual self that we use to anticipate outcomes and modify our actions accordingly. In that virtual world where we treat ideas as facts and then anticipate our actions, if those thoughts are partly or wholly wrong, then we may be mal-adapting ourselves to the facts around us. Someone may be adapting himself or herself based on the idea of a heaven, hell, or reincarnation. If those future outcomes are not real (and we have no reason to think they are), then the actions he or she takes may rob them of real alternatives that are better. Remember that when our minds are anticipating, they do not communicate with the body through language, but, rather, impulses. The impulses of fear can be triggered by fictions, like the idea of an intruder in your home when it's a family member or the belief in witches that led our ancestors to burn women alive.

Again, someone who isn't aware that identity is a useful fiction is forced to deny particular facts that don't suit his or her pseudo identity. I'm not talking about not knowing. There is much that is unknown. I'm talking about changing or denying obvious facts. Much of life's energy and attention is spent trying to be who we think we are and wishing for that to be satisfying. Unfortunately, this obsession with a fictional self is a way of life for many and continues until their deaths.

I invite people to inquire into reality, where people can speak the vulnerable truth of living and adapting to life's imperatives in changing circumstances. The responsibility and accountability that I'm talking about also includes life's ecstasy that's so often drowned in confusion and deceit. Many difficulties around sex are not about the act of sex. The problems are more likely to be things like: Who are we supposed to have sex with? What is normal? How often should we do it? What about marriage? Do we ask for sex or just allude to it through innuendo? Can we use sex as a weapon? Can we talk about sex and the fear of sex? The list goes on and on. There are problems with sex itself, but they are pretty simple and have to do with the mechanics of it. One of the paradoxically obvious, yet unspoken problems, of modern sexuality is that sex is used as a means to another end. It's not recognized that sex can also be an end unto itself. Sex is used to have children, get a spouse, prove manhood, grow spiritually, pay the rent, get attention, get a better job, keep your partner from getting mad, and get revenge. The list goes on. I don't mean to say that these things shouldn't happen. I am saying that we need honesty about such matters. If we use sex to accomplish something, then, obviously, it is a means to an end. Let's not delude ourselves with sentimentality. If we bullshit ourselves here, then there is little hope of getting to a deeper understanding of sex. If you are not sexual, then that is not a problem if you can be truthful about it. Before the pastoral revolution when humans started grazing animals, it's doubtful whether or not our ancestors understood the male role in reproduction. If that is true, then it means humans originally did not treat sex as a way to have children, but, instead, a simple instinctive joy. If that is true, then it means that consensual sex (when it wasn't a trade for something else) was simply an end unto itself. We need not recreate the ignorance of our ancestors to understand inherent value, something that is good for its own sake, as part of a good life. The same way that the beauty of a sunset, waterfall, or music, serving no other purpose, illustrates something good for its own sake.

Most of us have had painful experiences with sex and they can be obstacles to acknowledging our choices. Sometimes, the drive for sex dwindles for some reason, but celibacy is often just an identity, not the reality. One question is important: If you are in a sexual relationship and you aren't enjoying sex, what the hell are you doing?

I was in a group with a woman who told us an unusual story. Her mother lived in a retirement home. This lair of mostly retired women stood close to a park where homeless people gathered. Some of these women went to the park to find men to take home. They would give the men good meals, drinks, and showers and then fuck their brains out. You can imagine the looks on the faces of the people listening. They felt shocked and it took a few moments for people to recover. There was utter disbelief. I enjoyed the story, but felt sad because almost everyone listening either felt offended by the story or negated it. I suspect that most of the individuals listening would rather see these older women not having any sex than be participating in such conduct. There seems to be some weird idea that, after a certain age, a woman should cut off her hair, get a perm, and put herself out to pasture like a domestic animal to live the rest of her life babysitting grandkids, telling stories, and waiting to die.

I have repeated this story a few times and gotten the same reaction for the most part. All people, regardless of age, deserve a chance to live as fully as their circumstances allow. If life wants to dance with others sexually, then why stop it. These women in their 60s, 70s, and beyond possessed real moxie. They refused to live without the life affirmative experience of sexuality. They didn't have a lot of suitors standing in line, so they went where they could get what they needed. For the men, the sex may have been a means to a meal or an end in terms of pleasure. For the women, this park prowling sex seems an end unto itself. After all, it's not like these old widows wanted to start families. I suspect that some of these women probably didn't act this way in their youths. The closer one gets to death, the more a person begins to regret the things that he or she never did. I say, why wait until death is knocking at your door before you start to live?

When someone cheats on a spouse or lover, we often hear the dismissal of the sex because it 'meant nothing.' However, if it meant nothing, then why did he or she risk losing a wife or husband, home, and family? We know that this statement doesn't make any sense. I suggest that these people are really saying that the sex existed for its own sake. What does that mean? It means that sex is one of the things that, by itself, is part of a good life.

Here is another story told to me by my beloved Sharon. She was facilitating a women's group and, in this group, a woman in her 70s shared that her husband flatly told her "no more sex." She promptly moved into another room, put out a personal ad, and found several men who felt happy to lick her pussy. I say "right on!" It is so hard for many people to live the simple truths of their bodies. None of us can guarantee that life will afford us opportunities to enjoy our sexual capacities. If the same lusty old ladies mentioned two paragraphs above, and the woman above with her personal ad, had lived in Medina, Saudi Arabia, instead of Santa Cruz, California, their choices would have been quite different, regardless of their impulses. Women experience severe and even deadly punishment for going beyond the bounds of custom in backward countries. Such customs give rise in my mind to the question, "how much of the sexual behavior we see, arises from the dispositions of the people involved and how much is about customs with which they have identified themselves?" We should be adapting to the sexual circumstances and people around us in a mutually consensual freedom that does not impose arbitrary limits upon others.

Shame based on ideas about what we are supposed to be is crippling. I know, I have been there. The confidence to even ask for what we need and want is unknown to so many. Some of us hide in innuendo and beat around the bush, avoiding the responsibility that comes with speaking the truth. One thing is for sure, if you want to be sexual with another person, then you must take a risk. How do you know when you are taking a risk? When you're asking something and the other person can say no. That's when you are risking and taking responsibility. Telling someone that he or she is attractive is nice, but there is no real risk in that (although it may feel risky) because that is not a yes or no question. To flatter is sweet, and flattery is appreciated by some, but, if you want to be sexual, then chances are that you will need more than flattery. This statement goes for both women and men. Flattery is not taking responsibility for the sexual attraction. Flattery is often a way of trying to get the other person to take responsibility and initiate sex, giving another the opportunity to say yes or no. The idea of being rejected is so painful that many people simply go without if they can't find others to take the risk for them. I have heard "no" a lot in my life. I have also said "no" as well and, while I now regret some of those nos, there are also some that I don't.

I love to be adored as a man and I am not sexually interested in women who aren't turned on by me. I suggest that a "no" is better than a lousy sexual experience. Hearing "no" in regard to a sexual invitation will liberate a person's energy to seek other lover(s) elsewhere and, thus, I don't think hearing "no" is bad. It is just disappointing to hear. Why are some of us so terrified to hear it? If we build our identities out of our sexuality and look at "yes" or "no" as some evidence of who we are, then "no" seems to be a direct threat to our identities. If we try to build our identities out of relationships, then any uncertainty appears to be a threat and the quest for certainty is utterly futile. If your identity is built on the relationships that you are in, or want to be in, then you will suffer immense and unnecessary pain. It is only a question of when. The inability to realize our desires has a lot to do with fear, pain, and even the disillusionment of identity because the impulse to sexuality is often one of the strongest that we feel.

I doubt that we ever really meet another if we are trying to maintain an identity because we want the other to be a certain way so that we can feel okay about ourselves. In such cases, we imagine what it means about us to be with them. We never see the other as he or she really is because we see them as a means to sustain our identity. If I'm right, then many relationships are between us and what we think about the other, not between two human beings. We relate to our minds without knowing that is the case and the other is merely a screen for the projection of our thoughts. When we recognize awareness, then we can see the other, feel the other, recognize him or her as life in a person. Then, the meeting happens as something more intimate than a mental demand that another be some proof of who we are. Sometimes, such a living meeting is absolute bliss and devotion and, sometimes, it is a conflict. Yet, a life experience of real choice emanates from such an event regardless of the harmony or discord.

When we are free to come and go as we choose, then staying is truly our choice. There is room in life for countless demonstrations of benign sexuality and someone with a desire for the truth, whatever gender, is not a coward who runs away with his or her tail between his or her legs. There is a place for yielding and resisting, including our own unique display of life as an incarnation of matter itself, becoming conscious. After all, these bodies are matter. The trick is to not limit our capacities; to not be obliged by habits of the mind, such as our fictional identities or unquestioned views of the world.

NEW TANTRA

"We should not blame sex for our silly beliefs."

I am saying something different than most teachers because this book is not simply about learning techniques or trying to have spiritual experiences that will convince you of anything. Experiences happen, but achieving the 'correct' experiences is not essential to the recognition of awareness. This book includes welcoming and embracing all of the seeming paradoxes of life, such as creation and destruction, without denying one aspect of life to account for another. That means more than being able to say both yes or no to a particular desire. We realize not only that we can love and let go, we realize that we possess the capacity for murder without needing to murder anyone to see it. If we look selfishness in the face and disobey it, then selfishness is not our master. It is the inability to take responsibility for such human shadows that continues to haunt humanity by hiding destructive impulses behind ideals. We identify ourselves with good intentions and, at the same time, mop up the blood and squander the loot. In the less extreme case, we may lie to our lovers and deny them other lovers, while we, ourselves, cheat. That bit of selfishness is quite common. I'm not saying that we should give up our choices; I'm saying that we should let others have their choices because they don't live to serve our egos. This recognition of free choice for all makes the understanding involved here unique.

So much of what is sold as tantra or even spirituality is only rituals and techniques in different forms. One man wrote an article for a tantric web site in which he spoke of "doing everything with divine intention." Supposedly doing this practice would, somehow, help someone access his or her higher self or, as he put it, "tantric will." The idea present in his thesis was that through effort, you can somehow be different than you are, thus realizing the "tantric will." This tantric will is a goal-oriented achievement and what can be achieved can be lost. As if who you are right now is not capable of accessing your life's capacity. The only problem separating us from our freedom to choose among all our capacities is that we are fixated on some ideas about who we are and feel bound to the limits of those identities. If we try to be something different than the whole of ourselves, then we feel confused. Being ourselves would be trivial if we didn't habitually bypass that reality by mistaking a concept of self for who we actually are. The awareness that abides before, during, and after any achievement, regardless of being labeled spiritual, is what I am trying clarify.

There is nothing essentially wrong with any ideas, true or false, if we know that they are just ideas and this statement includes spiritual beliefs. Some spiritual beliefs are benign and help people, myself included. Most spiritual beliefs and practices are essentially processes of trading in old ideas for, hopefully, better ones. The problem with spiritual beliefs is that they don't awaken people to their awareness or the fiction of identity. Instead, these teachings send people on journeys chasing spiritual experiences. These experiences come and go, like all events, and when they go, people are left with their old habits, perhaps slightly modified. Then, all we can do is try again and again. In such spiritual gymnastics, there is no recognition of that which doesn't change through experience. No recognition of what experience is occurring in, I'm talking about our awareness itself. Awareness is nothing special. It is present in any conscious human, but the content of this understanding is different than if I were a teacher of some technique that merely altered states. That makes what I have to say different. You must judge for yourself if you decide to investigate what I'm saying, after all you are probably as capable of inquiry as I am. If you know that the seeking you've done has given you valuable experience, but that it didn't free you from your identity, or if you have never explored subjective inquiry before, then I encourage you to investigate what I say and evaluate it side-by-side with what others teach. This way includes inquiries into sex, but is not limited to sex. It seems clear that different people have different needs and I have noticed that there isn't much room for that exploration among particular groups of seekers. This closed-mindedness is a consequence of identifying with some particular teaching. Closed-mindedness often exists even among people who consider themselves to be sexually free. People are haunted by the idea of how things are supposed to be and, if they are not that way, then something seems wrong. This idealism is one cause of great suffering, even in the best of circumstances.

Teachings, both subjective and materialistic, establish a criterion of how things should be and, if we measure our choices by some criterion that hasn't arisen from our own lives, then there are bound to be problems. Biological evolution changes life and a chance variation that is better adapted to the environment gets passed on to the future to continue life. We are not outside that process. What if we possess a variation or an adaptation that has nothing to do with prejudices based on the past? If we judge such a variation through teachings only relevant to bygone ages and teachers who could not possibly understand today's environment, then we are simply being dangerously foolish. We are either ignoring all of humanity's progress or assuming that such progress is the responsibility of others. Our lives become sacrificial when we bind ourselves to the false beliefs of others.

"...in the matters which concern the shaping of our own lives, or the publications of our social opinions. In this region, we are not imposing charges upon others, either by law or otherwise. We, therefore, owe nothing to the prejudices or habits of others. If anyone sets serious value upon the point of difference between his own ideal and that which is current, if he thinks that his 'experiment in living' has promise of real worth, and that if more persons could be induced to imitate it, some portion of mankind would be, thus, put in possession of a better kind of happiness, then it is selling a birthright for a mess of pottage to abandon hopes so rich and generous..."

- John Morley

Even those rare people who know that they are living in awareness still have to live their lives, make decisions, experience the outcomes of those decisions, and die, just like everybody else. The difference between them and others is that, since they know they are not their ideas, they get to have their own lives. That is, they are not enslaved by their devotion to a fictional idea of themselves. Buddha left a teaching, Bodhidharma left a teaching, Kabir left his poetry, Ramana left his transcribed talks, Osho left countless books and videos, and Papaji left his recordings and videos. We are free to learn from these incarnations of life, but we are not to be burdened by them. If someone becomes bound by what I'm saying right now, then he or she has missed the point.

Life already contains whatever your capacity might be. Are you willing to take responsibility for it? What might you be capable of without the restrictions imposed on you by doubtful systems of belief? It is a powerful question to consider. The good news is that there are no requirements; you don't have to do anything you don't feel is right for self inquiry. I am encouraging an inquiry into your own awareness.

I do not wish to set up any concrete rules about sex or try to alter anyone's orientation (e.g., from gay to straight and so on). We should be vigilant to see if what we are doing sexually is destructive in any way and then amend our conduct or beliefs in order to render our instinctive drives harmless. I see limitations in popular beliefs about sex. I hope people disentangle themselves from such beliefs. If we can discover our sexuality in a way that is not deceitful, coercive, reckless, or violent, then there is no reason whatever for us not to enjoy it with anyone who wishes to join us.

The suffering around sex is immense and, regardless of what people do, it seems that others will disapprove. Such disapproval seems to be a source of problems. I consider the failure of religious commands an example that makes the point. Every person deserves to discover his or her own sexuality, provided that he or she doesn't harm others. I take this attitude toward sexuality to be one of my most important responsibilities to discuss. It is possible that I may hurt some feelings when I question beliefs and I wish that wasn't the case, but I don't know any way around it.

Perhaps an analogy will help you understand. In my non-literary work, I specialize in cleanups of people's property. I use a lot of dangerous tools and work alongside others. I try to never raise my voice when dealing with people. Indeed, in all the years I have done such work, I could probably count the times on one hand that I have used anger. If I see someone attempting to do something dangerous, I will yell at the top of my lungs, using anger or whatever seems necessary to stop any harm. In a situation like that, I am not concerned with the feelings of the other person; I am concerned with that person remaining unharmed. Sometimes, people don't always recognize danger. Their ignorance is innocent enough, but I have been driven to the hospital more than once because of avoidable stupidity. I don't feel any remorse about yelling, even though I don't like it. I've been yelled at too and it's shocking and hurts sometimes. I feel the same kind of responsibility handling both subjective inquiries and explanations about sex. I hope that the kindness intended is received by the reader. I live this human experience just like everybody else. It isn't easy. I have the ability to disagree with anything I have reason to doubt. I also hope that you, the reader, have that ability and, if you don't, I hope that you find it soon.

The manipulation of sexuality to serve a purpose is one of the most wounding and common practices that I know. A man I knew from a spiritual group died recently. His cancer progressed quickly. He really wanted to continue living. All of his life, he longed for a passionate sexual union. His wife couldn't or wouldn't meet him sexually for whatever reason and they both suffered within the horrible situation. I can only wonder why he chose to live that way. He spoke often about his suffering and felt guilty about his strong sexual feelings. He tried to be more 'pure,' meaning he struggled to not want sex, as if that would stop the suffering, but it didn't. After the cancer diagnosis, he faced a difficult reality. He asked his wife if they could try to have a normal sex life now that he was dying and she still couldn't do it. He died starving for the ecstatic joy of life merging with other people. He missed his chance.

It is a rare person who can say that he did not betray himself either for or against sex.

The man above denied himself and that hunger became a source of pain for most of his short life. His mind and beliefs wouldn't allow his body to behave naturally. He stayed married, feeling ashamed and at war with himself until he died. His widow took a lover shortly after his death, which I have no objection to. It seems as though there was a lot of unnecessary suffering going on due to ideas and it is sad that only death brought it to a close. I personally know and love a woman who offered to help him sexually, just out of compassion, but he could not receive that gift.

Perhaps an example from my own life would also be instructive. I have always been a sensual being. At one point in my young life, I concluded that the only way to get a woman to trust me was to suppress my sexual feelings for her, thus proving myself to be a 'good' man, worthy of her sexual favor. This crazy thinking seems to be somewhat similar to that of my deceased acquaintance and it's quite clear to me that some others think this way. The idea is absurd. I can't tell you of the misery that I went through with this strange morality. In the modern era, people talk a lot about sex, but living it in freedom is not as common as one might think. There are definite ideas in society about the way that relationships ought to be, typically these ideas are just old ideas with a bit of fresh paint. Trying to make oneself fit any idea is limiting, whether the idea is Victorian, new age, or libertine.

Regardless of where bad ideas about sex came from, what matters is that they are not adapted well the changing circumstances of our lives. I wasn't a prude by any stretch of the imagination. I think, perhaps, that I was so uncomfortable with my own intense feelings that I tried to make myself as respectable as possible in my conduct despite the fact that I spoke about sex loosely. Eventually, that idea went out with the trash. One would think that those individuals who consider themselves to be sexually open or free spirits would be free of such folly, but, in my view, it is not so. Speaking from experience, I have found that the spiritual rituals and techniques of tantra are, for the most part, arbitrary, along with many of the rules that people adopt to feel safe. We do not manage anyone else's affections. People practice the techniques that come from presumed sexual authorities with the hope that they will have new experiences, feel closer to God, live longer, learn to have sex without dysfunction or guilt, create love and intimacy with their mate or mates, and/or master transcendence, among other benefits. I don't doubt that, for most people, these intentions are sincere. Yet, even with good intentions, a person doesn't necessarily become liberated. What usually happens is that individuals become identified with the practice or the experiences that they generate. Fortunately, for many people, this kind of sexual inquiry allows for some new experiences beyond the limits imposed by their cultures or convention.

Meditation and spiritual practice serve a purpose in that they invite people out of their ordinary habits of mind. They reveal that life experience is bigger than they previously imagined and that is a good thing. There are difficult to label, mind-boggling, body sensations that are experienced through these practices. If one hasn't undergone that type of experience, then discussions about such an experience become difficult and almost useless. An uninitiated person can't see beyond his or her own habits of mind, so anything else seems imaginary. I know people who have apparently undergone similar experiences without formal help; their openness is amazing because it isn't tied to a teacher or teaching. However opening ourselves to our inherent capacities happens, it is good as far as I can see.

Once people are initiated beyond their habits of mind, we might think that awakening would be a natural progression, but that is not so. The spiritual rituals and techniques used and the experiences that they produce become a new center of identity. If a person experiences openings and phenomenal, psychic, or energetic (un-labeled sensations) novelties, then that person may feel self-satisfied that they are evolving. A person may feel that he or she has awakened. I experienced that situation before actually recognizing the awareness in the midst of all passing experience. For example, as a teenager, I meditated daily and, on one occasion, I felt three days of showering bliss and joy for no reason. I thought that I had transcended, but, as with any experience that has a beginning, it had an end. My experience changed and faded to a memory. Such experiences often inspire people to go deeper into the technique, breathe constantly with the belly, enlist the aid of spirits, and become more mindful, all methods that are presumed to be the solution to whatever caused the experience to fade. The thinking is that "if only I could do these kinds of things constantly, I could maintain the experience." This bullshit is the worst kind of all of the kinds of bullshit that exist. What goes unnoticed in all of these esoteric gymnastics is the awareness that this experience is occurring in; that is consciousness itself. It's being conscious of the inner spaciousness from which all experience arises. This awareness is the you that remains before, during, and after any experience. The reason that this awareness might be missed is that the events occurring within awareness get all the attention, and the awareness that is the neutral consciousness is simply there in the background, like the sky behind clouds.

I'd like to recount an example of a spontaneous, non-ritualistic event that occurred some years ago. I was traveling in India and met a beautiful young woman, Kara, while we participated in a tantra group in Pune. We became lovers. The context in which we met seemed wild by any standard. Despite the fact that we both had lovers outside the group, we soon became more involved. We shared many adventures and hard times traveling across India.

One night, Kara had a date with an ex-boyfriend. I asked another woman out on the same night; she accepted, but then canceled at the last minute. I resigned myself to go home alone. Out for a walk, I stopped by a German bakery to get a cup of tea and I saw a woman who also participated in the tantra group. I considered asking her to spend the night with me and then decided not to and started home. I felt a bit uptight because the reason I didn't ask her was fear. She was also a friend of Kara, which could mean opening an emotional Pandora's Box. Moreover, I didn't want to be rejected in my longing. If this woman said no, then there would be the pain of rejection and, perhaps, harsh disapproval. If she said yes, then there would probably be pain because I would speak the truth to Kara. I felt bitter allowing my fear to decide my fate. I realized that I didn't have to obey the fear, no matter how strong it was, and I could say what I felt. I would have to live with the consequences of my actions either way. I turned around, walked back to the bakery, got her attention, and asked her if she wanted to spend the night with me. After a long pause, she asked about Kara. I explained to her that my beloved was on a date of her own and probably having a great time. She said "yes" and we went back to my flat.

I met Kara for breakfast and asked her about her date. She reported making love and joy with her ex-boyfriend. I felt vulnerable listening to my lover talking about another man after sleeping with him. She asked about my evening and I told her about my night of making love with our mutual friend. She blew up in my face. Certainly, I wasn't prepared for such a reaction, after all, she had slept with another man the night before! We argued from breakfast until the next morning. Finally, we got down to the idea causing the hurt. She was frightened that I would leave her for another woman because I slept with another woman. It felt contradictory for a woman who is into tantra and felt sexually free enough to sleep with another man to have such a fear, but she did.

We had to deal with this fear, live in denial, or end our relationship. I felt manipulated and betrayed because of the obvious double standard, but we got through it carefully and respectfully. Then, we discovered that our love for each other felt strong enough to face this emotional pathos again if it arose. Indeed, that wasn't the last time it came up. Just because people are into freedom with regard to sex, doesn't mean that it isn't painful at times.

I'll digress briefly to talk about authors. One of the problems with listening to an authority speak is that the authority often omits the distasteful parts of the story and speaks only of the attractive parts that serve his or her own interests. This decision is pragmatic and tends to make the authority look like a saint.

The way the story with Kara ends is not ideal. We both had to go home at some point. She lived in England and I lived in America. I had extended my trip and was running out of money. Saying goodbye felt excruciating. The ominous separation emotions mixed with passionate sex and, as it turned out, I missed my plane as a result of my bewildered state.

Back in America, a few months later, I began to fall in love with a friend who also happened to be married to one of my closest friends. We had known each other for more than 10 years and, of course, it was a difficult situation. Their marriage appeared to be over and, after careful consideration, we decided to become lovers. The three of us, Sharon, myself, and Sharon's husband of 27 years cleared the air. I am happy to say that we don't hate each other. In fact, we share a lot of good will.

After Sharon and I had been together about a year, I went to England for three weeks to see Kara. I didn't want to leave Sharon, but I also felt the need to be with Kara. I spent a month with Sharon before I left trying to reconcile her feelings of fear and uncertainty without much success. I felt determined to go. When I got to Europe, I found myself trying to reconcile Kara's feelings as well. We had a great time, but she also felt used because the meeting didn't lead to anything beyond itself. We spent many nights talking, crying, and making love. Although I wouldn't leave Sharon for any reason, Kara hoped I would return to her and she professed to love me no matter what. Still, the joy of that meeting overflowed and I remember it to this day. I'm glad I didn't miss it. Kara and I are still in contact. If anyone judged my meeting with Kara as a means, then it was terrible, but if anyone judged it as an end, then it was joyful.

I felt terrible when I stepped back to look at the event, seeing two hurt women. It's true that some of that pain arose from their ill-adapted beliefs, but I could have also done better. The whole event caused pain to everyone involved. I felt love for both women and I wished that the distance wasn't so vast between Kara and me. After a long pause, Kara and I began talking again and both of these women remain in my life.

There are painful moments in everyone's life. Generally, pain is judged to be bad or wrong. The mind tries to reconcile the pain by creating all kinds of stories about the pain and how it could have been avoided (e.g., "If I had done something differently, then it would have been okay."). These stories have a certain plausibility with regard to learning from pain, yet they are hypothetical and don't really have anything to do with what actually happened or the results. These stories remove us from the present and keep us in the fiction of what might have happened or what should have happened. If we become caught in these stories, then it is not possible to respond to what is actually going on. Being stuck in our mental narrative is like painting a picture of the world in our mind, using our concepts as the paint and then mistaking that mental painting of the world for the world. If we take that representation of the world in our minds for the actual world, then we are lost in our own mind. We may not get out. As a result, we are irresponsible to life because we are bound up in our stories about life and the emotion induced by those stories, while simultaneously remaining blind to the limitations of our concepts.

The events with Sharon and Kara described above happened after I realized that formless awareness is part of any experience regardless of any thought or perception that comes and goes. I could have simply avoided the pain by fixating on the awareness where there is infinite peace and no problems. However, because I understand that identity is a fiction, it is precisely that reality that makes it possible to enter into any experience profoundly, including pain or joy. There is no reason to avoid a painful or beautiful reality and, if one is not avoiding it, then one can respond to the actual events; hence, the term 'responsibility.' Pain or any experience, pleasant or otherwise, demonstrates what is untouched by any experience. What is untouched by any experience is awareness itself. It is like gold that you can shape into a beautiful statue of a divine image or a demon. Whatever the form, it is always gold. The awareness is the gold, not the forms that come and go. We need not pretend that the demon statue isn't ugly. The experience wasn't bad or wrong. Sometimes liberating lessons come in unpleasant forms. Self-realization is not only about awareness, but also adapting to life. Many teachings exist that suggest awareness as an escape from life, as in ascetic practice, as if such an escape were even possible. We don't need to escape from life to stop manufacturing misery. Awareness with our capacity for action repressed or renounced is not living freedom, it's as if we neuter our responsibility and become a crippled eunuch who hides from the uncertainty of life. If we run away from life to be free, then we are not free. I realized this reality, but I wasn't practicing some technique or ritual. I wasn't trying to be anything other than what I was truthfully. I hurt two women I loved, which doesn't seem all that lofty. I am grateful to these women. This event was a painful, spontaneous experience that increased my understanding of a conscious life. I'm aware of limits, but not bound to the limits needed to sustain a fictional identity.

If a person only identifies himself or herself with the pleasant or 'good' aspects of being, then there is little possibility of being accountable. To those of us who've been taught to think that enlightenment is only peace and transcendence of life's problems, we've learned something mistaken and I'm prepared to discuss that mistake. Awakening is transcending the fictions about ourselves in the midst of life (not apart from life.) Awakening is inclusive, not exclusive. If you don't believe me, just look out your window long enough and life itself will demonstrate it's inclusiveness to you. It might a spider that shows you how ruthless and unsentimental life can be. At least animals do not hide the pain that they cause behind some high-minded ideal. Life is not what obscures awareness; identity obscures awareness. Awakening includes the peace of formlessness, but is not imprisoned by formlessness either. Awareness exists within the midst of all experience. Awakening includes everything that arises in that formless awareness. Everything! To recognize ourselves as awakened is a part of responsibility because our choices are no longer arbitrarily limited to the attempt to sustain any fictional identity.

A SEXUAL PUZZLE

The problem of taking refuge in ideas that cause us useless pain motivates me to write. I am limited in that I write primarily in terms of heterosexuality, but I do not mean to leave out any benign sexual impulses. I think we human share many of the similar problems and pains, but they happen in different circumstances. Of course, some forms of pain I don't know. I don't know the pain of white racism from the point of view of a minority or sexism from the point of view of a woman. I can only extrapolate from the injustices I do know.

The problem of creating misery is different from problems that are unique (e.g., to those beyond the pale of arbitrary social norms). I want to acknowledge the great courage of the LGBTQ community. What members of this community endure due to the cultural rejection of their sexuality is terrifying and profound. The courage and tenacity to stand up as unique sexual beings is often exemplified in of this community.

When someone is unfulfilled sexually, he or she hungers and this fact doesn't discriminate. Being who you are as a sexual being is not easy for anyone. I endure distrust and personal attacks for being non-monogamous and people have tried to disgrace both me and my lovers. Regardless of what people think, I'm true to my life impulses. It is a tragedy that living beings act as if trapped in deference to social disapproval often resting on questionable and even false beliefs. I lost three friends as a teenager to suicide. My heart aches to use them as examples of unrequited longing and I can't prove that unmet desires caused their suicide. I can say those desires were a source of pain for them. There is a lot more capacity for joy including sexuality than we often get to live in our lives. Unfulfilled instinctive impulses become a source of suffering, especially if we assume the reason we cannot live out our desires, is that we are somehow unworthy.

The problem of identifying ourselves with experiences is that we create useless misery among other profound sensations in our minds. For example, we might instantly change our lives forever by doing something like going south, changing our names, and never looking back. Not that it is a good idea mind you, but the point is that our capacities exist right now, for good or bad and we forget that we have this power to change our lives and the lives of others. The reason we forget is because many of our capacities exists beyond how we habitually think of ourselves. It is one thing to be stifled by circumstances beyond our control and another to be stifled by beliefs.

Let's discuss dicks and pussies. So many arbitrary ideas exist about these organs that it is almost unfathomable. How big is it supposed to be? Is it tight? Is it dirty? Is cum gross? Is it supposed to smell that way? Are you circumcised? Is it okay to kiss someone down there? How often should I put it somewhere? Where can I put it? What about inanimate objects? If I like that pleasure, does it make me bad? The list goes on and on. One thing is certain: what can be done sexually is done sexually, with and without accountability. This abundance of possible sexual conduct also includes doing nothing and, for many women and men, the most painful thing that happens is nothing. I've spent I don't know how many hours listening to people lament about how their husbands, wives, or lovers won't meet them sexually. Sometimes, disappointment happens even if the couple is having a lot of sex. It's difficult to explain to a partner that sex isn't right when they will agree to do anything you ask sexually. I know a woman whose husband accused her of being a sex addict because she wanted more sex than he felt willing to give. Their sexual relationship existed only on his terms and, if she tried to initiate sex, he would reject her. She told me that she wished she could reject him when he wanted sex, just to get even, but she felt afraid, having no guarantee when he would want sex again. She would take what she could get, like a beggar. Some folks change the subject when I suggest that they tell their spouses that they either need more sex or that they need to find a lover because they feel like they're dying on the vine. They are missing things that are part of a good life. It seems that deceit or divorce is preferable to such honesty. Another option is to let the starvation become routine and think of it as 'the way it is.' This is bowing to fear and life-denying beliefs. I know men and women who don't want to share their lovers with anybody else, as if a lover belonged to them as property. I know men who have more than one woman, even more than one wife, and they acknowledge their own instinctive impulse to live this way as something that makes them feel like they are really living well. Some aspect of them would be suffering if they limited themselves to one woman. I've asked some of these men if their women could have more than one lover and the answer was often emphatically: NO! How these men avoid remorse for the women who are suffering that arbitrary limit is beyond me. I know of a love triangle where the exact opposite is true. The woman can be with other men, but she forbids the men from being with other lovers. The men involved are madder than hell about this double standard.

The above are examples that show how we can be terribly selfish and unloving to one another, while being accepting of our own instinctive joys. Such selfishness robs others of good things that life might offer them, as if the reason they exist is to serve our beliefs and purposes. If we act selfishly with others, denying them good things, then we treat another human being exclusively as a means. In such a circumstance, we do not see others enjoying a good life as an end unto itself. Let's stop rationalizing not allowing others the choices life may offer them, especially if we want similar choices for ourselves. Perhaps some accountability for the pain caused to the other person will, in turn, cause us to lighten up. Those people who feel the need to lie to their partners and live a hidden sex life outside of their relationships cause distrust and pain. The moral bargaining chip for indulging in deceit is usually guilt. The guilt becomes the penitence, sort of like going to confession. We don't have to be accountable for what we do, if we feel bad enough about it. We feel cleansed by using pain like a bar of soap. Some of us justify dishonesty because we feel angry or denied sexually. These reasons are plausible, but do not erase the deceit. If you are in any kind of closed sexual relationship and you are not having sex, then what the hell are you doing? Assume you are in a committed relationship and the woman or man you are with is unfulfilled. If you can't give that person what he or she needs, yet you refuse to let him or her seek it from someone else, then you are a sadist. It is akin to learning that your partner is hungry and you not only deny him or her food, but you also say that it isn't okay for him or her to seek it someplace else. We don't all have the same appetites or metabolisms. Sex can be a life-affirming, sustaining, worthwhile experience. If you deny someone you love that joy, then I seriously question your love.

The word 'love' has been so misused that it seems to have lost its meaning. People love their cars, countries, or mayonnaise on French fries. What about love of people? Do you think you can love only if you feel safe and secure? Sorry, love isn't safe and secure. If it lasts, great, but if you try to make love serve your ideas of what love is 'supposed to be,' then I would suggest that you are in a relationship with your own mind and, perhaps, not even seeing your partner, except through a vision of how you think he or she ought to be. One thing is certain: nobody can live up to an idea for the simple reason that people are not ideas. People have needs and desires, and those needs and desires include the instinctive impulses given as a part of being alive. The impulse toward sexual joy is something that we inherited from the first cells that began to divide in the primordial soup. Sexuality has nothing to do with any idea about it and it exists regardless of any ideas.

The dichotomy of heart vs. dick and pussy is particularly difficult to see and quite vicious. A presumption exists that the emotional heart is more wholesome and pure than our genitals. This idea seems supported by advocates of old time religion and some forms of therapy and pop spirituality. Opposing life's impulses in a way that creates useless misery may lead people to nurture some aspects of themselves, while neglecting or hiding others. Some people seem only slightly affected by this lunacy, while others are crippled by it. If you try to reject the sexual needs of your body, then the body will probably try to meet those needs in some other way. The sexual biological imperative is so important that it is almost impossible to deny. Sexual denial is exemplified by the forced celibacy of priests. Their perverted sexuality displays itself to us in many strange and malevolent ways. It is amazing to hear people say "I can't believe a priest would molest a child." That statement suggests that such people believe it is actually possible for a human being to walk away from a biological imperative. Perhaps, a denied impulse turns to greed, to bitterness, or into the crass smile of a lecher, which will make your skin crawl. However the perversion comes out, a preoccupation with sex almost always exists, even if that preoccupation takes the form of fanatically criticizing and negating sex. Consider moralists who decry as wicked any kind of sex outside of their tradition. Sexually repressive lunacy directly impacts and robs the next generation when religious people stifle sex education.

I've known many people who suffer one or another form of belief that is not well-adapted to their lives, including beliefs about sex. Some of these people continually go to therapy, workshops, and spiritual events where the interaction is heartfelt and sentimental. At such gatherings, people receive a lot of attention, like validation of their feelings, hugs, and a collection of listeners who discuss the difficulties of not being sexual. The problem with such discussion and support is, in spite of such workshops and seminars, some individuals who feel a struggle with their sexuality might spend years 'working on themselves,' during which time, their habits of thinking about sex may change only a little. I don't think that is what they need. People who feel themselves dying on the vine due to sexual starvation need more than hugs. Sadly, some of us haven't found many positive sexual experiences, although I suspect that most of us would like to. The pain being discussed might exist indefinitely and wasting time at a workshop where little changes is itself depressing and often expensive. Some people don't have 30 more years to explore their sexuality. They are in danger of missing an opportunity to experience sexual unions with others for the simple reason that they don't have a lot of time left on the planet. Some people use their age as an excuse. It usually sounds something like this "Nobody wants to be sexual with an old lady or man. I'm too fat, too wrinkled." These statements are bullshit.

In my mid-20s, at a celebration put on by tantric folks in India, a woman in her 70s approached me, touched my bare chest, and kissed me on the lips. She took a step back, looked me up and down, and told me that I was a beautiful man. I looked into this woman's bright blue eyes and began to wonder how I could take this woman home without causing my beautiful young girlfriend, Kara, who was also at the celebration, too much pain. I took too long to find an answer and, before I knew it, this woman left with a man younger than me!

Age and looks are a lousy excuse for not being sexual when there is a world full of people who would be willing to be sexual if given a chance. The question is usually not if sex is available, but will we accept sex on the terms offered in our lives and is that sex both worthwhile and benign. It's a mistake to assume emotion is wholesome and sex as something less than that. I don't think there is anything wrong with emotional support. To me, emotion is intimately connected with sex. However, emotional experiences can't be substituted for sexuality any more than water can be substituted for food. The analogy has its limits because one would starve to a miserable death quickly by substituting water for food, whereas substituting sentimentality for sex may cause years of misery. I don't care how loving emotional support may be, there always seems to be cruelty hidden in the kind of caring that avoids sexuality. The struggle against benign sexual satisfaction often involves reality loss. Life in harmony with facts including sexuality is divine because it is not delusional. Sexuality held with intelligence and adapting that sexuality to the facts of our life, is a human being in harmony with his or her own sexual impulses.

If the sexual union was a hindrance to awakening, then I could not have awakened. I simply recognize awareness as the foundation of all experience, wild or mild. We have no excuses to keep on identifying ourselves with passing events and continue dream walking. If an excuse remains, then come hang out with me and we will see if we can't destroy that excuse.

Tantra is not just limited to sexual experiences. Any conscious embracing of life and the senses, including opposites, is tantra. For example, when a person meditates and experiences himself or herself as the formless witness, then he or she is also a body, with a mind, that exists in time and this sense of self is an event that is occurring within that witness. This witnessing is a paradoxical meeting of form and formless. When I say formless, I'm not implying mysticism. Instead, I mean only awareness and such formless awareness exists implicitly in all experiences that we recognize.

"At the start of sexual union keep attentive on the fire in the beginning, And so continuing, avoid the embers in the end.

When in such embrace your senses are shaken as leaves, enter this shaking.

Even remembering union, without the embrace, the transformation.

When vividly aware through some particular sense, keep in the awareness."

Excerpts: Vigyan Bahirava Tantra, (approx.) 2000 BC

I would note that the advice above is to remain in the awareness not the passing senses.

Most people have experienced being angry with a person for whom they really care. The love and anger certainly don't cancel each other out and, in the midst of this emotion, a person must bear the friction, which sometimes makes for heated and intimate interactions. People can opt to consciously (not automatically or habitually) embrace these seemingly opposite emotions as a part of life. Tantra embraces life, including not getting what we desire. One of the methods to realize our awareness from ancient tantric scripture is to become totally involved with a desire and then quit the desire before satisfaction. If we cannot step away from a desire, then we are slaves to desire. We would be fools to say we have willpower unless we also have the will to stop it at any time.

Sometimes, life's circumstances will place our impulses at cross purposes. We want the food in the fridge, but we suspect it's been kept too long. The desire for food is life affirmative and the desire to avoid getting sick is also life affirmative. There is no need to deem one impulse good and the other bad because they both serve life.

I am always impressed by the straightforwardness of some bold and non-traditional personal ads (i.e., people who stand in the reality of what sexually moves them). The problem I see is that there is little, if any, recognition of the awareness that their experiences occur within. There is little, if any, encouragement to recognize awareness and without that recognition we tend to get identified with what we do, what we think, and what we feel. For example, if we identify with the body, then when the body changes a disillusionment of identity will ensue. Let's live in and enjoy these bodies without being imprisoned by identification.

When one is awakened, that awakening reveals itself in every aspect of life, not because everything is done consciously without recourse to habit or routine, but because no habit, routine, or event becomes an identity. An awakened person can be wrong; make mistakes; become angry, horny, or sad; or do anything that a human is capable of, but they are simply not identified with those things.

Again, we cause useless suffering by identifying with both the wonderful and terrible events of life. That identity is a powerful oppressor, not only of sexuality, but of many of our capacities. Some people fear that, if they recognize and normalize their sexual impulses, then they will they will be unable to control their desires and their impulses might take over and devour their lives. Indeed, sexual obsession happens just like earning money can take over a person's whole life. I suggest this obsession is about people identifying themselves with their sexuality. Identification is both dangerous and painful because we seek to do the impossible (i.e., secure and sustain fictitious identities). This whole consideration may seem scary in part because society uses threats to our fictional identity to control people. If we are not aware that the idea of the self is a fiction, then, like it or not, we react to any threats to that fiction as if our lives or well-being depended on it. Take the case of spiritual seekers, they are often identified with what they do. They may have known profound, non-typical experiences through meditation or some other spiritual practice and they may consider themselves highly evolved. At the same time, they may ignore their own tendencies that don't fit into their spiritual identities. They actually play the same identity game as someone who identifies with money and property, only the game is spiritual prestige in the spiritual marketplace.

YOU ARE THE CRITERION

Why you? As you are right now is the only place your awareness can exist. The point should be trivial except that we simply ignore the fact. If awareness did not exist, then no chance of awakening would exist and we could not have the discussion. If you become self realized right now, then it would be you, exactly as you are and any fictional self would be realized as just a concept. One of the problems of traditional and non-traditional paths of awakening is that whoever started the path or teaching becomes the criterion. Take Buddha as an example. If the person who is the catalyst for any particular teaching is dead, then, usually, exaggeration exists in regard to the story of that person's life. The ordinary person can't hope to live up to this exaggeration. If the catalyst of a particular teaching is alive, then people often try to defer to, impress, or imitate that person and these scenarios often lend themselves to creating a new spiritual identities instead of seeing those identities as fiction.

Often a spiritual or therapeutic guide will ask the seeker to go deeper into who he or she really is, but this urging drives the seeker into his or her past or trying to be who he or she thinks he or she ought to be based on the ideas advocated by the authority. If this person does awaken, then he or she may find that living his or her realization is different from the teaching, causing conflict to arise with the teacher. It may seem easier for us to stay confused than to disagree with someone we acknowledge as an authority, especially if we believe, rightly or wrongly, that this teacher helped us. Gratitude inspires loyalty whether the teaching or teacher possesses integrity.

When we awaken, when we rely less on unconscious habits, when we stop living on autopilot, life remains unpredictable. Life is wild, whether it is conscious or merely automatic. Let's begin to take responsibility in ways we've never dreamed of before. Not only are we not identified with our habits of mind, but we can consciously disobey any of these habits when they are no longer necessary to sustain our fictional identities. We are not threatened simply by being in the unknown, which is quite often the case.

The collective mind is a type of herd mentality involved in popular wisdom. Here, the criterion isn't oneself, but the number of people willing to agree something is true. As if groups of people haven't been wrong, even for generations. We have all seen examples of suggestibility, and undeserved deference in other people; seeing this flaw in others is easy. The difficult part is seeing such poor reasoning in our own thinking. We may be giving authority to a group and the group may be giving authority to an individual who is unfit to lead. It may serve here to give an example. I know a man who considers himself to be an authority on dieting. His weakness and ill-health are obvious and startling. How can he imagine that he is an authority? Where did this authority come from? Well, he read some book written by "somebody who knows." What this man doesn't realize is that any fool can write a book. There are many books about proper dieting and, if he looks, he will find contradictions among them. This poor fellow can't understand the reality staring back from the mirror, which suggests that 'something ain't right.' I suggest that the authority over his own body, which is his birthright, is something he cannot take responsibility for because he accepts another authority and identifies himself with that teaching.

It would be one thing if deference to an unworthy authority only affected the individuals who are overawed, but that is not the case. I imagine some Christians discussed witch burnings after publicly viewing such an event. I wonder how many lay people believed in witches just because the authority told them to do so. In any case, no good reason existed to believe in witches and, still, countless people suffered and died for nothing. I could give many examples of people placing their trust in dubious authorities in the realm of modern spiritual make-believe (e.g., people who believe in abundance myths who give their money generously to some cause thinking that some god or the universe will reward them for so doing). Sometimes, beneficial circumstances coincide with such beliefs and make the general belief seem true, but those circumstances are subject to change. I've seen this change take place among believers in the middle of remarkable good fortune and watched those people continue to be generous, under the guidance of a spiritual authority, until they lost their money and had to stop out of necessity.

A person must accept responsibility for his or her own being. If we do grant authority, then we can take it away if we have reason to do so. The one who grants authority is the judge. He or she possesses the ability to strip others of authority. People who will take responsibility for their own value judgments seem rare. Typically, we explain away the flaws and weaknesses of authority; their mistakes are simply excused, which is one of the reasons why there are so many seekers and so few people who wake up. All people who awaken to the reality that their concept of self is a fiction also accept responsibility for their own being. We can't pretend to be who we are, we can only pretend to be who we are not. I may appear in some ways to set a standard of how to be, but that is only one way. Life is not as redundant as people like to think. No awakened person imitates another. That is not freedom in action, that is following a preconceived course. Our own life is the criterion. In awakening, we establish the criterion for authority and any granting of authority is provisional based on our own judgments. Why would we give another authority? Usually, we do so because we think some other is more adept at solving a particular problem than we are, but, if we build identities out of our relationships to authorities, then we are screwed as the problems of identity remain.

The defense of a fictional identity causes great confusion, but the varieties of discontent caused by mistaking that identity for who we are, such as despair and confusion, provoke our desires for more understanding and new experiences. These impulses are not bad, they are the engines of life adaptation. Problem-solving provokes our investigation into both the outside world through science and the inside world through science and introspection. Unfortunately, we tend to run away from the awareness of appealing ideas to get away from any confusion. The fact is that all our seeking is an attempt to be better adapted to the real world, which includes our ideas about ourselves. Whether we are wandering across India or putting a bet down on a craps table, we hope for something better. However, it is easy to fall into error. Life itself becomes more aware through us. The question is: What will we find when we realize that the limits in our lives are not the same as the limits of our self-concept?

The life that began on this planet as a single cell that divided into two has made a long journey through evolution and is incarnated in each of us. I don't have any idea what your life might be for you and I can't say that it should look like mine. That is for you to discover exactly as you are, including your life's problems and your personal flaws. When we deny or reject some aspects of ourselves, we deny or reject some aspects of life. The idea that some aspects of reality are sacred, while others aren't, is one of the primary sources of separation from our own realization. Don't get me wrong, some aspects of being consciously alive are incredibly difficult, painful, and ugly.

One of the most popular archetypal images symbolic of consciousness is the statue of Shiva dancing. The circle of fire around Shiva signifies creation and destruction. I am not advocating Hinduism, but I suggest that the image of Shiva is more insightful than most ideas about consciousness and self-realization. Most people consider that the beautiful things in life are sacred and anything destructive or ugly isn't. This idea is often a mistake and is, at best, situational. The point here is to be clear about what we can or cannot change. Earlier, I wrote about a man dying from cancer who struggled with living his sexuality and felt haunted by a terrible deprivation all his life. He made his sorrow about not having a sex life public and sought solutions as his death approached. Out of compassion, one of my lovers offered to give him sexual comfort since his body, at that time, was still capable of joy. He could not accept this act as a gift and continued to struggle with his wife in a sexual desert of his own making. He died in that desert. Life offered him an alternative and he rejected it. I suggest that he rejected it because it did not fit his preconceived ideas of himself.

It helps to be around a person who understands the freedom from your ideas of self, but not if you must subordinate your impulses to the authority of the other. If you subordinate yourself, then that act disrespects the life that shines in your own eyes. It becomes the subordination of your life to some other life. The guru tradition is rife with philosophies that prescribe deference to teachers, ideals, and questionable scripture. Life reaches out through us into our own circumstances, that is an entirely unique set of facts that we as individuals have the responsibility to adapt too. Think of two seeds blown in the wind. If one roots in good soil and the other in the crack of some concrete, the life in each must adapt or perish. If we subordinate our life forces to an authority, then we let another take the responsibility and we don't get to live our own awakening. To reject freedom while in pursuit of freedom is a contradiction hidden in many spiritual teachings that have the seeker serving the teacher or teaching for years, perhaps a lifetime, without ever realizing that the concept of being a seeker, that identity itself, is a fiction. Many people hang around gurus for years and never wake up, even though they give to the teacher or teaching everything they have to give, literally. I suggest that they give something they should keep: their own authority about their own lives. I am not saying that a person shouldn't accept help. I am saying that a person should get to decide if he or she is, in fact, being helped. Without this responsibility, we cannot distinguish between wasting our time and time well spent investing in something helpful. This judgment becomes more difficult if the teacher insists that the problem is the seeker and that the seeker suffers from delusions and must trust more. If you lack confidence in your own understanding and ability to criticize any teaching or authority, then it is possible that you may stay inert for a lifetime listening to others who seem to know more, but are really exploiting you.

My beloved Sharon tells a story of her bad experience with an authority. A woman acting as her teacher left Sharon feeling constantly abused and her teaching wasn't producing many benefits. Most of the people associated with the teacher deferred, which created a feeling of an individual against a crowd. The school had a hierarchy and the teacher's own guru accepted the narrative of the abusive woman, not because it was true, but because of her position in the school! As it turned out, this woman chose to use her power to flatter herself instead of liberate people. It was necessary for Sharon to criticize this woman and, when she did, the conflict ended a 20-year relationship. The amazing part of the story is that Sharon had a realization that shattered her previous identity and opened her eyes to see the trap of identification. Sharon also exposed a woman who used her status to aggrandize herself at the expense of others. It is my opinion that this teacher possessed a profound rhetorical power, what seekers took to be spiritual power (i.e., siddhi), but the teacher hadn't realized that her own identity wasn't real. Her charisma, which was attractive to seekers, became a trap for the teacher herself. She remains, to this day, a bitter woman who surrounds herself with those individuals who believe that they are inferior to her. She is able to surround herself in this manner, in part, because she continuously reminds them of their inferiority contrasted with her apparent wisdom. This misguided teacher is trapped in her own identity. That is not awakening.

I am not saying that the help of a teacher should always be painless. I am saying that the help of a teacher should liberate you into a better understanding of yourself and the world around you. We want less and less reality loss and more and more reckoning with life on its own terms. The criterion for that success is not words, authority, or scripture, but rather our own lives. In lives of freedom, we need not deny or alter facts to maintain mental identities. We understand that reality loss (i.e., taking thought to be more than thought) comes with a terrible price. If we know someone is helping us, then we may consciously seek his or her help to speed our disillusionment regardless of the fact that it is painful. We defer only on our own authority. Let's understand that any illusions come with a cost, kind of like credit. The longer it takes to apprehend the facts, the larger the cost in terms of time that we won't get back and energy wasted on what is unreal.

Delusion is a more painful alternative to the truth because life constantly threatens to burst through at any time with its brutal and undeniable facts that care nothing for our beliefs about ourselves and the world. It is better to face the problems of what exists than waste our time in fictional problems. Real help fosters improved adaptation to the real world. Real help involves the truth that, regardless of the limits of our understanding, we are never separate from the facts of life. If a teacher isn't liberating us into the facts of our own lives, then what the hell is he or she doing?

It is extremely helpful to see a person who is not trapped in identity when he or she is angry, sad, busy, or relaxed. We see him or her when he or she is going through the same types of stuff that life throws at all of us. However, we also see that this person is not suffering the anguish of trying to make a false self real. The idea that awakened people don't go through similar human experiences just because they're awake is absurd. Awakened beings are free to live their lives, eat, feel emotions, go to the bathroom, get sick, and die, just like everybody else. Their recognition that identity is a fiction shouldn't be defined with their experiences. The gift of any awakened person is that he or she is not mistaking himself or herself for a fiction. They have limits and make mistakes just like everyone else, but they are not identified with these shortcomings. They need not deny their own faults. The trick is not about having the right kind of identity, but seeing identity as only a fiction. The awakened one is simply life staring you in the face through the eyes of another without being in the prison of identity.

I once heard a wise man say that "the awakened one gives you what you already have and takes away what you don't have." The disillusionment of my identity is the awakening I discuss and I don't believe that I would have awakened without the help of three people: Osho Rajneesh, H.L. Poonjaji who I will refer to as Papaji, and one American whom I call the charlatan. In any case, that is how my awakening happened.

I would like to give credit to those individuals who have helped me. The first person is Osho Rajneesh (formerly known as Bhagwan Shree Rajneesh), who showed me, through meditation, that the world contains many experiences outside of what I knew. I could dance outside of the identity that is my past. I thank Papaji, who pointed me to the awareness that remains every time identity dissolves "like a salt doll in the ocean." I give thanks to a charlatan, a man who I won't name. I don't want to give him free press and he serves as a bad example. This anonymous man perceives me as a political threat, and I am. This man, inadvertently, helped me. You see, I gave up the last vestiges of my identity as a seeker to see this man for what he was. I stood against him and his community. I am grateful to all of these teachers. I began writing this book, in part, to expose his methods of deception.

It also needs to be said that my awakening stands on its own. I do not feel the need to agree about anything in particular with those individuals who helped me. My gratitude doesn't make me a cut and paste copy of someone else's realization. I stand on my own ground.

How does one become the criterion? I can tell you some of what I discovered and maybe what I say will resonate with you. Desire the direct understanding of awakening; that is the disillusionment of identity. We may obtain all the ornaments, regalia, beads, titles, and respect of being a great seeker and wear the robes of a sage and still be deluded. We must never reject facts. To turn away from facts is to enter a vicious circle. It is only a matter of time before illusions fall in front of the truth, better sooner rather than later. Surrender to the facts of life that shatter any of our beliefs. Beliefs are not who we are, including beliefs about ourselves. I think a world where we are not creating fictional suffering and spreading it to others is a better world than one where we create useless misery. Dogmatic belief is cheap and it stops all self inquiry because the answer is already given. If we discover, in our own lives, that something we were told is true, then it is really ours, not just some borrowed idea. Let's admit what we are really capable of and then decide what calls to us in our own lives. Perhaps you, my dear reader, will shine a new light that exposes a hidden self deception or mistake, perhaps the fruit of your life will make a better world than it would otherwise be. We live in a society that has many problems to solve. Our solutions will lead to new problems. We need all the clarity and help we can get. Every person who ever contributed to humanity bloomed on the same vine that sustains you. That vine is life itself and it extends back in time to the first cells that began to replicate.

CONSCIOUSNESS

As a seeker, I sought, from spiritual offerings from different teachers and traditions, the creation and, more importantly, interpretation of altered states, what people call spiritual experiences. I did not see the limits of that identity as a seeker. Papaji possessed an insight into my problem. I asked Papaji a question about meditation. I had meditated for many years and flattered myself due to my uncommon experiences of altered states, I mentioned that fact in a question to Papaji. He looked at me with his big, dark eyes and said "What is this name you have written on this question?" I told him it was pronounced Manadeva, a name given to me when I became a disciple of Rajneesh. He said that it was a bad name and, without asking if I wanted a new one, proclaimed me Gyan Deva. I thought "Fuck you! I'm here asking a question and you want to change my name! Who the fuck are you?" What I learned from that meeting was that I knew nothing about the consciousness he tried to indicate. I learned my meditation practice had far less value than I thought because my focus had been on the experiences, not on the consciousness present in all experiences. The rest of the conversation exposed me to my own spiritual idealism and, at the same time, began to expose the fiction of my identity. I felt agony.

I tried hard to get what Papaji said, but every time I would answer one of his questions, he would become more enraged with me and yell "NO! YOU DO NOT UNDERSTAND!" You see, I interpreted everything through my past and could not get even a glimpse outside of what I believed to be spiritually beneficial. My answers exposed my ignorance. I left feeling totally defensive.

After that meeting with Papaji, I thought about all of my spiritual experiences over the years and how impressed I felt with all of that. I experienced deep gratitude for the benefits I received from my spiritual practice because my life improved a lot from it. I feel a great deal of loyalty to anything that has helped me. I also thought that those experiences meant that I was progressing in my spiritual evolution. I considered leaving satsang with Papaji. Many people present at this first conversation between him and I felt shaken by it because of his ferocity. They felt glad it was me and not them getting the slap. I thought "I'm outta here, man. I should go get laid back in Poona." Still, something was haunting me about Papaji. I decided to stay a few more days and give Papaji a chance. Meanwhile, I came down with amoebic dysentery and experienced incredible physical pain; I was shitting my pants in public. I also had scabies. I couldn't be sexual with my beautiful lover because I worried I would give her the dreadful little bastards and the dysentery made me too weak to be virile. If you put all of this together with the disillusionment of my spiritual identity, then you can imagine that I felt weak and vulnerable with nothing to console me. I went to Papaji. In the royally fucked condition that I described above, I had my first understanding of awareness sitting with Papaji. I recognized awareness as something not bound by the experience that occurs within awareness. I felt such struggle wanting to cling to who I knew myself to be and the spiritual experiences that I had chased for years. The experiences that previously seemed evidence of my identity simply dissolved as my mind fell silent. I'm not saying that this gift of clarity was virtue on my part; it's like something seemingly hidden in plain sight became obvious. The recognition of identity being vapid happened in the midst of friction with the orientation of Advaita; that is to dismiss all phenomena as unreal, even though that teaching recognizes experience as a form inside our awareness. We can dismiss identification with experience without absurdity, but to dismiss experience itself is a misunderstanding, as if we could negate experience.

I became clearer about my own awareness when back in the U.S. I went to sit with Gangaji (a disciple of Papaji). Her understanding really spoke to me and helped me. The great teachers of the Advaita path teach "do not abide in the mind," which is a great way to get a glimpse outside of the habitual ideas about ourselves. The great thing about the Advaita understanding is that, in this tradition, the teachers, like Ramana and Papaji, and the living representatives of this tradition, like Gangaji and Isacc Shapiro, speak beautifully about formless consciousness. These teachers are not tantrics (they may do wild things, but they don't express it as part of their teachings), so their transmission is not clouded by difficult rational, ethical, and empirical considerations. Only vichara (i.e., self inquiry) is on the menu. It is a pure teaching. It has great value and I am grateful for it, but it is too pure, as far as I am concerned. Consciousness cannot be falsified or contradicted. No risk exists in discussing it and, as long as one focuses on the often unnoticed awareness, no controversy exists. However, it is consciousness in the midst of problem-solving, while adapting to new circumstances that serves to improve life. It's not life itself that is unreal, but a life that is symbolized in the mind as something unreal. If the world were truly unreal, so would be the recognition at the heart of the teaching of Advaita. The teaching itself would be unreal because it arises in the world.

My original misunderstanding born of Advaita was as if I had lived two lives: one as a conscious awareness and one as a body and mind that needed to work, eat, love, sleep, argue, etc. We cannot separate awareness from any experience and to insist that awareness itself is the only thing of value is like gouging out one eye. It took a few more months for me to recognize that all experience, both the truth and the mistakes, come and go within awareness, so there is no reason to reject any experience that comes and goes. We need not identify ourselves with it. When we recognize awareness, we begin to see the stuff of the mind for what it is, only thought.

My interest in the experience of life hasn't left me since I realized awareness. We should remember that any discussion of awareness like I'm having now must be conceived in awareness and that seems circular. There is no way to dissociate from the mind and talk about anything, but if we remember that any discussion of the awareness of self is just passing thought and that the awareness itself is not bound to concepts that rise and fall, then this recognition puts any thought in it's rightful place. No need exists to fuss about desire. Once a person is awakened, he or she need not reject the mind, desire, or experience of any kind that includes beautiful and uncomfortable experiences like fear, sadness, joy, pleasure, or making a mistake, all experiences dance in awareness. The dance is not bound to be nice. It can be horrible. Even still, the awareness that is the consciousness present in all experience stands free in the midst of all transient events. I am here to say that you are that same awareness, like it or not. The question is "Are you ready to account for all of who you are?"

I would like to say a little bit about how awakening has affected me as a person. I still have a body-mind, yet I am utterly different. I am doing all the things that I need to do to survive in the world. I own my own business and also do birthday and holiday entertainment in costume. I play drums and have been taking music lessons for years. I am [at the time this was originally written] currently going to a community college. It is now 2:05 a.m. and I am writing this piece. I love to relax with friends, travel, and have fun. I live a human life with my own unique way of living in discovery of this life. What I do or don't do does not affect my awakening. The conscious nature is simply holding all that is occurring. When I first started to experience myself as present with, but not identified with, experience, my body went through some changes in sensitivity.

I experience the suffering of the world in a different manner. For example, every time I start my car, I help to poison the environment. I'm embracing the defects of humanity in a new way. The life in others is not so different than the life in me, like the ocean taking the form of another wave. The creative, sustaining, and destroying forces of life affect me as they do others. The people I am around must also reckon with these forces in me, which can be wonderful and difficult. If you asked my beloved Sharon what it is like to live with me, she would tell you that it isn't all bliss. Not even close. I welcome and enjoy the intimacy of sexual relationships. Speaking personally, I'm quite okay with the people I love staying or leaving, but that does not mean I don't feel it. The feeling is not a threat to identity because identity is only symbolic. I'm willing to meet life on its own terms. In a way, this awakening freed me into being ordinary.

If we think that awakening will get us out of anything, then we are clinging to a half-truth. Awakening gets us into everything as well as gives us choices outside of our past ideas. I'm saying that awakening explodes arbitrary limits. I experience all of the emotions that any human is capable of; I am probably more sensitive than I have ever been. I have no reason to think I am especially capable or incapable of what a human can do, good or evil. I am a body, an animal with instincts. I have been experiencing spiritual, energetic, or unlabeled somatic phenomena all of my life in various forms, particularly after I began meditating, but these altered states are no longer a fetish. I occasionally share some of these experiences with people, but I have a bit of a pet peeve regarding such matters. There is such a fixation on non-typical experiences and people mistake these things as a criterion for human evolution. I do not wish to send someone down the path of chasing experiences when his or her freedom exists right now in spite of what he or she may think.

We don't need to see auras or feel great movements of unidentifiable sensations for self inquiry. When we hear about these things, we can never know whether the one speaking is telling the truth or is lost in imagination. Assuming that what people say is true, we don't know what those unlabeled experiences mean. We are just as much an incarnation of life even if we experience none of these things; having or not having experiences is not a barrier to your self-realization. Identification with experience is the barrier and our identity is of less substance than a soap bubble. Identity is only the ephemeral stuff of thought.

I eat meat. I spent a lot of years experimenting with diet, including being vegetarian, and vegetarianism doesn't suit me. Vegetarianism is not an identity, but I admit that it is probably much more sustainable than eating meat, which has a greater environmental impact. I make mistakes. I'm not afraid of mistakes because there is no concept of self to defend. This boldness in the midst of mistakes is one of the reasons that awakened people can be so unruly. I am free to do anything because I know who I am and who I am is unaffected. Paradoxically (that means I can't reconcile the contradiction), I'm affected as a human being and being aware makes me take responsibility because it hurts when I hurt others. Taking responsibility doesn't mean that I don't hurt others or have flaws. Responsibility is being with the reality without pretending. If we pretend, then we won't have access to choices beyond the limits of our imaginary identities. Sometimes, my choices require a strong stand and, sometimes, an apology. Whatever the case, when I feel an impulse, I can follow or disobey it; sometimes, that impulse is admitting I made a mistake. If I feel the need to allow someone to rage at me, then I will stand and receive it with a vulnerable heart. If I understand that there is an injustice being done, then I will try to put a stop to it one way or another, which may require something besides being a sweetheart.

When I first got a whiff of myself as awareness, I was ruthless with clarity. I wasn't accounting for how I affected others. If I didn't like my experience, then I could just direct my attention to the internal quiescence where all thoughts rise and fade. Someone once made fun of me, calling me "consciousness on the march," which translates to "you are rejecting the human limitations of life's experiences for the limitlessness of awareness." I came to understand that to reject any aspect of life is to reject the chance to adapt to that aspect of life and there are often better ways to do things than what I have done in the past. I didn't understand at first. Awareness is unaffected, so why would anyone want to return to the world and its inherent uncertainties? The reason is because there is no place else to go. Why tear awareness away from the world when it is uniquely adapted to the world. I could say in one moment "whatever happens is perfect." I could also say in the same moment that "the way things are really sucks" and be referring to the same thing. The aspect of my being that doesn't like the way things are is also coming and going in awareness. If a person has just an inkling of his or her conscious nature, then all he or she will have to do is look to see that consciousness is present and free, even in the midst of the most beautiful and the most hellish human experiences that come and go.

I love the juice of life. When I make love, I connect with the life of my lover. Love of truth is the best way to honor the love and life we share because anything less taints the love. Love of truth is the only divinity I accept. That love of truth admits both limits and errors when it is true. It admits to desire when it is true. I may feel the impulse to honor my lover with words; I may talk dirty. The desire to surrender or to lead may arise. Sometimes, I become so ecstatic to meet another unbound by identity in a sexual embrace that I can't describe it in words. Anything a body is capable of is possible for me because the arbitrary limits of our self-concept have no hold. Consciousness itself liberates my inherent intelligence and creativity. These things have natural limits and I can hold my own genius and naiveté without it becoming evidence of any identity being real. I am free to know what I know and to not know what I don't. There was a time when those things were both in doubt. I see the life in others, which has made me more functionally human than any therapy I've ever done.

It seems to me that I could have easily missed this paradoxical self-realization in countless ways. After all, it is easy to identify with the body or mind because it is surrendering to a habit. We can hold our capacities and even conflicting impulses, though it is not always easy. To sense unbounded possibilities for love and creativity, and wake up with bad breath is not an easy paradox to hold. I don't feel the need to impose my understanding on anyone. I had to give up all of my ideas about awakening in order to meet this awakening as it is.

THE SACREDNESS OF WORKING AND MONEY

Finally, I repeat that the desire for truth is the only thing worthy of the name 'sacred.' All the gods and scriptures can fade into the vagueness of history for the sake of the desire for truth. What is true is better adapted to the reality of life and this recognition places life itself above the ways we conceive or explain life. No teaching is the linage, not Christianity, Islam, tantra, Advaita, Buddhism, or any other means to an end. All of these things occur in life and can pass away and life still exists. Life is the real linage and we are a part of that! As a result of this understanding, any of our flawed explanations can be replaced by better explanations. Respect for life includes improving and sustaining life, which brings me to the topic of work and money in life.

To many people, the subject of work excludes higher morality because it is never separate from being simply a means to another end. However, that ethic treats work as often something separate from life, which seems absurd. The emotion around issues of money is such that to speak of money at all is like poking a stick into a hornet's nest. The ideas that money is filthy, money is the root of all evil, and work is a burden are prominent. These ideas are rooted in particular facts that may have some plausibility, yet are oversimplified and don't help anybody. Most of the time, this type of thinking becomes an excuse for why life is unsatisfying. Blame is pointed away from oneself. The idea that money is the solution to all problems and that work is a source of identity is also limited and limiting. Becoming fixated on work or, conversely, to be fixated on avoiding responsibility will drain off energy and attention that could be used for self inquiry and living a good life.

We can become so bound in the struggle to survive and trying to escape that struggle that not much is left over. I am not saying that a person can't awaken if they're poor or rich; that has nothing to do with the recognition that the concept of self comes and goes in awareness like clouds in the sky. However, the fixation on some particular aspect of ourselves to the exclusion of others prevents us from seeing even obvious things around us.

You probably won't awaken without self inquiry and if you are bound in a struggle to survive, then you probably won't be able to give yourself to inquiry. You will still be formless awareness in a form. Regardless, you will not be separate from awareness in any experience. The body-mind occurs in nature and is subject to the laws of nature (i.e., creation, sustaining, destruction), but formless awareness is that from which the phenomena is consciously experienced.

The paradox is that free awareness takes form as these limited bodies. These bodies are the formless life in form, therefore, that which sustains these forms honors life and it is through sustaining these forms that awakening and awakened life become possible. It is work and money that feeds and sustains these bodies and, if you aren't paying the bill, somebody else is. The story of Ramana (i.e., an Indian seer) is significant here because, at one time, he chose to devote his whole life to inquiry and sat in meditation without seeking food. If the people who passed by Ramana hadn't put food in his mouth, he would have died and the world would have missed the gifts of his self inquiry, which he shared with Papaji years later. Those individuals who fed Ramana were either working people or survived off the labors of others. Whether they had purchased the food or grew it themselves makes no difference. They fed Ramana, he lived, and others benefited as a result. Their work sustained life and that sustenance extended beyond themselves.

If you are lucky enough to have people put food in your mouth so that you can devote your life to realizing what is true, then you are a fortunate person and it is a desecration of that generosity to take it for granted. For many of us, being sustained by others isn't a possibility. We create our sustenance by selling the fruits of our labor or services.

Whatever the case, if you want to inquire into the nature of being, then you will need to sustain that which creates the opportunity to do so, and that takes money. Work sustains life.

If a person can't hold or save money, then he or she is sort of like a person who can't hold a sexual charge. As soon as the charge begins to build, he or she expels the energy, kind of a financial, premature ejaculation. This financial problem is a difficult habit of mind to take responsibility for because of plausible excuses for why the financial struggle is the way it is. I have known these excuses well. The results are financial impotence and struggle. I am not talking about the tragedies that occur that drain a person's resources, such as an illness. I am talking about the inability to create resources to be drained by such an event.

If you are interested in the choices I advocate, then I hope you have a functional financial life so necessity does not drag your attention away from self inquiry. If you are relatively stable, you can maintain a degree of independence and will have more courage in the face of opposition. It's easier for someone self sufficient to question commonly held beliefs than someone who must run with a crowd to earn his or her daily bread. If you can't deal with the facts, money, conflicts, and paradoxes that are inherent within the realm of the everyday working world, then I suspect that the paradoxes of more choice may be more than you are ready for. Financial responsibility roots a person in his or her physical reality. If you are not fact-based in this way, then I would suggest developing this skill by opening a savings account and, without fail, contributing at least 10% of your net income to it. This savings could change your life and there are more ways than one to save. I've known many people who so exhausted themselves making a living that other things of which they were capable simply went by the wayside. My above statement was only a suggestion, kind of like someone suggesting you get off the train tracks when the train is coming. It is to your advantage to not be stubborn.

CONCLUSION

Regardless of where we might agree or disagree, I thank you for reading this book. My hope is that I've illustrated the problems and habits of mind, including identification and disillusionment, as well as the solutions of self inquiry, freedom of choice, and self-realization in a new light. I hope you now realize how the creation or discovery of altered states is not itself proof of anything other than the fact that halting your habits of mind or body routines will, of course, cause you to experience yourself in a new way. If you now add even a grain of salt to any interpretation of altered states offered from any authority, then I declare this book a success.

Your life and experiences must be quite different from mine and you may have arrived at a different understanding than I intended. That is quite as it should be. You blossom on the same vine of life as me and I won't underestimate what life might accomplish through you. I'll just remind you one last time that quieting the mind won't cost you anything and couldn't possibly hurt you. Perhaps, we will meet one day and, if so, I hope to know how this book has impacted you. You have my warm wishes for your life discovery and joy.

NOTES

1 Desiderius Erasmus, The Praise of Folly, Translated by John Wilson (Clarendon Press 1925).

2 "The curiously underwhelming reaction to the Wright brothers first flight," Financial Review, 3 August 19, 2015. http://www.afr.com/lifestyle/[1]

3 "When Homosexuality Stopped Being a Mental Disorder," Psychology Today, September 18, 2015. https://www.psychologytoday.[2]

4 Reay Tannahill, Sex in History (New York: Stein and Day, 1982), 46-48.

5 John Morley, On Compromise, (Macmillan & Company 1886), 236.

---

1.   http://www.afr.com/lifestyle/arts-and-entertainment/books/the-curiously-underwhelming-reaction-to-the-wright-brothers-first-flight-20150812-gixaom

2.   https://www.psychologytoday.com/blog/hide-and-seek/201509/when-homosexuality-stopped-being-mental-disorder